GREENGOWN

David Kinloch is from Glasgow where he grew up and was educated. He is the author of six collections of poetry, most published by Carcanet Press, the latest being *In Search of Dustie-Fute* (2017) which was shortlisted for the Saltire Prize. He has degrees in French and English from the Universities of Glasgow and Oxford and spent much of his working life as a teacher of French at university level. In 2003, he changed course to focus on the teaching of creative writing and after retiring in 2019 is now Emeritus Professor of Poetry and Creative Writing at the University of Strathclyde. In 2022 he received a Cholmondeley Award in recognition of his work to date.

BARBARA. — Je lui ai demandé, il a refusé net-
rétement. Mon mari est d'une cruauté mentale ter-
rible.

LAVERNE. — Est-ce vrai, madame, ce que...

BARBARA. — Notre divorce ? Hélas...
Je suis venue en France pour divor...
France, je n'y ... tarder, ...
Quand je ... je veux qu'on ... enterre.

LAVERNE. — ... parle plus de cette affreuse
chose.

BARBARA. — ... Tout est arrangé, n'est-ce
pas, Maroussia, ... d'abord qu'on jette mon
cendres du haut ... avion, suis-je déjà été fait.

Ainsi star américaine ne s'est init enterrer en
France : j'espire en la première... Dans très long-
temps, bien entendu.

Achille a appris, ... sedia et le champagne.

OUSPARSKI. ... verre de vodka. — Longue vie
à la merveilleuse ... la plus belle, la plus
importante de toutes ... the world.

BARBARA. — Merci, ... Rome, monsieur
Ouspaxski ?

OUSPARSKI. — Oui, par ... puis je suis
Arménien, on pistolé j'étais ... été franchisé
naturalisé Français.

BARBARA. — la France !... que...
LAVERNE. — ... je connaisse mon ...
BARBARA. — ... oui, Biarritz, Cannes, ...
Pâris, Deauville, ... des trucs ...
... pas ...

OUSPARSKI. ... y voila.
... mais être faire tourner
Oraw ... Votre ... ora dit que ...
avec ... avec la Métro ce ...
voudr ... Axacaine. En ce ...
un ... extraordinaire pour ...

OUSPARSKI. — ... faire la prod ...
France. Je voud ... qu'à Berlin ...
qu'à Berlin, je vou ... Hollywood ...
imaginer sa production ...
que Barbara Bow ? V ...
français avec le secret ...
verrons.

BARBARA. — F ...
Marie le lira.

OUSPARSKI. — Je ...
célèbre... Je l'ap ...
deux collaborateur ...
Bulgares qui ont ...
vivait Kinofascan ...
j'engage Kid Stirling ...
ferons un film français ...
au monde le vrai visage de la Fra ...
propre, ea nonchalance, sou apparent ...
cache une foi très grande dans sa vérit ...
Nous autres, Français, puis ne savons par ...
des qualités du notre race ; je veux faire un ...
cher, nous, bien ..., réir et nef comme no...
drapeau.

Lavarie ... a ... cette except...
... progressé, de peur ...
... à l'heure, bonnot une ...
Bulgares ... romaric. Loin ce ...
Philippe I...
... appelle Larvi ...
Raymond Lar ...

OUSPARSKI. — Qu'est-ce qui vous prend ?
LAVERNE. — C'est fini. Mais ça valait ça, avouez-le :
bravo pour le complet.

... Les autres se regardent entre eux.

... EBE. — Il est un peu piqué, ce bonhomme.
OUSPARSKI. — On un peu ivre.
BARBARA. — J'ai cru que mon mari était entré.

... — Il joue de la trompette ?

... — Oui, de temps en temps, sans raison.

... — Je comprends alors que vous vou-
... en France ne vous déplaît pas ?
...achille et Émile sont qui apportent leur
... fruits. Le visage d'Ouspaxski s'illumine en
... le voit mélodrent Achille et Émile, portant
... se relèvent. Ils passent près de Laverne.

ÉMILE. — Comment la trouvez-vous, monsieur ?

LAVERNE. — ... peu difficile.

ÉMILE. — Oui bien ? On ne croirait pas, à la
... qu'elle ... courir la foule !

LAVERNE. ... parisie de sa côtelette. Elle se
... moi ... aboient les haricots verts.

... c'est la côtelette première, mon-
...

... Une seconde, n'est-il pas été de trop,
... Je vais la réclamer à la cuisine.

EBE ... Mol, de la voir de près, ça me fait un
drôle d'effet !

LANE. — Remettez-vous.

OUSPARSKI, qui voit Laverne parler à Émile. — Qu'est-ce
qu'il peut-on ... raconter à Émile ? (Appelant) Émile !

ÉMILE. — Monsieur ?

OUSPARSKI. — Que vous dit ce monsieur ?

ÉMILE. — Oh ! rien, nous parlions de Madame.

OUSPARSKI. — Allez plutôt à la cuisine me chercher...
... vous avez oublié.

... Oh c'en Achille qui, sonn à l'heure, revient
... des fa... suite.

LAVERNE. — Alors, chère madame, le principe de
... tourner en France ne vous déplaît pas ?

BARBARA. — Au contraire, voyons. Mais laissez-
... prendre mes vacances, ensuite nous verrons.

OUSPARSKI. — Vous partez toujours demain pour
le Côté d'Azur ?

BARBARA. — Oui, Marie a retenu les places. Au
... Marie, avez-vous téléphoné chez ma couturière ?

... — Vous arrive dit que vous la feriez.

BARBARA. — Oh ! j'ai oublié. Vite, Marie,
darling, allez ... téléphoner tout de suite.

... — Le téléphone est...
... dans la cabine ... Marie entre
... la cabine.

... — Marie !...
... hein, c'entrait pas à La ...
... vous ouvrir la cabine ?

... — Bien robertines, par...
... — Mademoiselle, on vous appelle.

Marie sort, tenant l'appareil de la main.

BARBARA. — Marie, dites bien que, si on n'a pas

GREENGOWN

DAVID KINLOCH

NEW AND SELECTED POEMS

CARCANET POETRY

First published in Great Britain in 2022 by
Carcanet
Alliance House, 30 Cross Street
Manchester, M2 7AQ
www.carcanet.co.uk

A CIP catalogue record for this book is
available from the British Library.

ISBN 978 1 80017 279 1

Book design by Andrew Latimer
Printed in Great Britain by SRP Ltd, Exeter, Devon

The publisher acknowledges financial
assistance from Arts Council England.

CONTENTS

for Eric

GREENGOWN:
the loss of virginity in open air; sod,
turf on a grave.

– John Jamieson,
Etymological Dictionary of the Scottish
Language

DUSTIE-FUTE

When I opened my window and reached for the yoghurt cooling on the outside ledge, it had gone. All that remained was a single Scottish word bewildered by the Paris winter frost and the lights of its riverbank motorways. What can *dustie-fute* have to say to a night like this? How can it dangle on its hyphen down into the rue Geoffroy L'Asnier where Danton stayed on the eve of revolution? How can it tame this strangeness for me or change me into the cupolas and flagstones I so desire yet still notice every time I walk among them? Does the 'auld alliance' of words and things stand a chance among the traffic and pimps in the Publicis Saint-Germain? For it's not as if *dustie-fute* were my familiar. I could easily confuse *dustie-fute* with *elfmill* which is a sound made by a worm in the timber of a house, supposed by the vulgar to be preternatural. These words are as foreign as the city they have parachuted into, dead words slipping on the sill of a living metropolis. They are extremes that touch like dangerous wires and the only hope for them, for us, is the space they inhabit, a room veering between dilettantism and dynamite. Old Scots word, big French city and in between abysmal me: *ane merchand or creamer, quha hes no certain dwelling place, quhair the dust may be dicht fra hes feete or schone.* Dustie-fute, a stranger, equivalent to *fairand-man*, at a loss in the empty soul of his ancestors' beautiful language and in the soulless city of his compeers living the 21st century now and scoffing at his medieval wares. Yet here, precisely here, is their rendez-vous and triumphantly, stuffed down his sock, an oblique sense, the dustie-fute of 'revelry', the acrobat, the juggler who accompanies the toe-belled jongleur with his merchant's comic fairground face. He reaches deep into his base latinity, into his *pede-pulverosi* and French descendants pull out their own *pieds poudreux*. Dustie-fute remembers previous lives amid the plate glass of Les Halles. They magnify his motley, his midi-oranges, his hawker lyrics and for a second Beaubourg words graze Scottish glass then glance apart. In this revelry differences copulate, become more visible and bearable and, stranger than the words or city I inhabit, I reach for my yoghurt and find it there.

DUSTIE-FUTE IN MUMBLES

I get up in the night
and let his voice out
of the breakwater into light.

Pier upon pier constellates
in the lyre of his memory:
jetties tensing at the touch of boys' feet
which echo in his mind like ships
that nudged his severed head, bobbing now
in my swivel chair like a buoy.

Dustie-fute released from the Oregon
pine of Mumbles pier, tells me
of mushroom anchors, jarrah wood paving
of Dundee and how at Arromanches,
locked within mild steel pontoons,
he took the weight of tanks.

Post-Eurydice, he has floated in
to tell me of the sex of words
which looped around his ears
among difficult Scottish kyles,
setting *aucht* upon his lips,
froe and *huzziebaw* in his hair.

He has come to tell me how domestic loss
placed a cypress in his heart,
its tongue half-learnt and half-inherited
which gave fast stories that surged in him
like lifts, sharp swords that hung above his head.

He has come to tell me of an underwater
tongue: hippocamp, useless
as the moles and dolphins
which burrow and porpoise
only in arcades of pleasure
they bear upon their backs.

GURLIEWHURKIE

*Unforseen evil, dark, dismal, premeditated revenge. It is scarcely possible
to know the origin of terms of such uncouth combination and indefinite
meaning.*
Etymological Dictionary of the Scottish Language

Habbacraws! The Renfrew Ferry throws up its glass bonnet.
She nods. Tonight she sails: black fisher of the Clyde. Far out
beneath the Kingston Bridge an illegal on-deck banquet cups
its ears and jumping to its feet says: 'Can you hear them? I
hear people in the air, but cannot see them. Listen!' We strain
(with every pore) until we hear invisible brothers, whole words
against our flesh. And they are: *greengown, dustie-fute, rinker,
rintherout, set, abstraklous, alamonti, afftak, baghash, amplefeyst,
let-abee for let-abee.* It is dew on Gideon's fleece. It is Homer's
bounding, flying and consequently alive words. It is Plato
thawing in the Glasgow air. It is the head and lyre of Orpheus.
All these and on the deck before us whole handfuls of frozen
words, gay quips, some green, some azure and some gold. Shall
we fear them then? Take no risks and we'll get no slaps! One
of us begins to horde, yet warmed between our hands they
crane upwards like a baby cham. It's then the gurliewhurkie
gets to work: just as we're about to understand their throats
are cut. *Mump the cuddy, aftercome, falderall* and *ezle* melt on a
lover's palm and shout: *hin, hin, hin, his, tock, tock, bou, bou, bou,
bou, tracc, tr, trr, on, on, on, on, proddle, proop. Habbacraws!* We
saw them look back over our shoulder into the water. We saw
the words stop bobbing like so many buoys in the water. We
saw the last gleam of dark eyebrows in the water and it said:
by-coming, bairnie of the e'e.

THE REV. ROBERT WALKER SKATING ON DUDDINGSTON LOCH

after Raeburn

The water tensed at his instruction
and trout gazed up at his incisive feet.
We felt that God must be in clarity like this
and listened to the valley echo
the striations of his silver blades.

Far out on Duddingston Loch
our true apostle sped
with twice the speed
of Christ who walked on waves.

We saw him harrow ice
with grace of the elect
and scar the transubstantiation
of wintered elements.

With a sense of real presence
he crossed our loch.
What need of vestments
with such elegant legs?

THE LOVE THAT DARE NOT

Even the illness that extinguishes it comes in borrowed clothes, not one name but many, forming the syntax of your end. Unravelling its hidden meanings, side-stepping tears that dare not fall yet because they would admit the last page of this dictionary has been turned, I trace you back, nudging you, as I used to, from word to word:

The days you called me *rinker*, a tall, thin, long-legged horse, a bloody harridan, I called you *rintherout*, a gadabout, a needy, homeless vagrant, like the tongue we spoke beneath the sheets. Our life as mobile and happy as the half a dozen Scottish verbs I'd push across a page on Sunday afternoons, trying to select a single meaning.

Here it is: under *Ripple* or *Rippill*, a squat paragraph which tells us we must separate the seed of flax from the stalk, undo our badly-done work, separate and tear in pieces. And when we are birds, must eat grains of standing corn, when clouds, open up, disperse, clear off. Its noun has you in its grip: an instrument for rippling flax.

Or you might find us under *set* which seats, places hens on eggs in order to hatch them, assigns work, settles, gets in order; puts milk into a pan for the cream to rise, sets fishing lines, works according to a pattern, plants potatoes, makes, impels, includes, besets, brings to a halt and puzzles, nauseates, disgusts, marks game, lets, leases, sends, dispatches, becomes, suits, beseems, sits, ceases to grow, becomes mature, stiffens, congeals, starts, begins, sets off

the love that dare not   Except that now, so near the end, when I would like to hold you and have been forbidden, I search for it in your eyes, daring their definition.

From the window of the Hardie-Condie Cafe, I see the ghost of a rich friend of my grandmother drive down Forfar's Main Street in a Rolls Royce I was sick in as a child. Behind me the watercolours of stick girls walking through trees are misted blobs percolating in coffee steam. Mother comes in like Scott of the Antarctic carrying tents of shopping. The garçon brings a cappucino and croissants on which she wields her knife with the off-frantic precision of violins in Hitchcock's shower scene. Soon I will tell her. Show her dust in the sugar spoon. Her knife gouges craters in the dough like an ice-axe and she tells the story of nineteen Siberian ponies she queued behind in the supermarket. Of Captain Oates who boxed her fallen 'Ariel'. The chocolate from the cappucino has gone all over her saucer. There is a scene and silence. Now tell her. Tell her above the coffee table which scrapes with the masked voice of a pier seeming to let in some waters, returning others to the sea, diverting the pack-ice which skirts around its legs. Tell her a fact about you she knows but does not know and which you will tell her except that the surviving ponies are killed and the food depot named Desolation Camp made from their carcasses keeps getting in the way. From this table we will write postcards, make wireless contact with home and I will tell her of King Edward VII Land, of how I have been with Dr Wilson and then alone, so alone, in day-blizzards just eleven miles short of the Pole and ask her to follow me. I am afraid she has been there already. She smiles like the Great Beardmore Glacier and goes out into the street with stick girls to the thirty-four sledgedogs and the motor-sledges. You are too late. Amundsen is in Forfar. She has an appointment. Behind me I can sense the canvases, the dried grasses pressed into their grain like eczema on an open palm. Later I will discover her diary and what I told her.

Hush-a-baa or *huzziebaw*: *a* lullaby *from the verb to huzzh. S. Pron with so strong a sibillation that it cannot properly be expressed in writing.* Clips attached to the H and W enable you to fasten it around your head as with all middle-alphabet words. Select your preferred definition by pressing firmly on the hyphens: impelled by the see-saw of its own intimate history, huzziebaw will balance between your eyebrows and take over:

mantelpiece clocks in the fragrant Dinard light tick past you like lemons on an old fruit machine: *hush-a-baa.*

aluminium trolleys forward and reverse in the quiet green hospice: *huzziebaw*

the landscape steadies and you see a young man lying with purple marks all over his thin body, a mother and sister kneeling, a man who is his lover, poised, and a photographer, crouched. We are all waiting. This is huzziebaw. And you wonder: surely the closed curtains swaying in the summer air will bring forth something: ease, a scrap of melody, a brittle word that will not simply say the pain of this last lullaby but be it, blinding us beyond the reach of the camera's ultimate, pale cut.

WARMER BRUDER

A slang expression, literally 'hot brothers', used viciously of gay men in the death camps of Sachsenhausen and Flossenburg.

I

Concentrate hot brothers:
shovel snow with me
in Sachsenhausen
from one side to the other
and back again.

Then in the silence
make an angel of the snow
which falls unceasingly
on camp and foe.

The lights of Grangemouth
dance their triangles
into tears,
its smoke the ghost of blood,
the melting snow.

II

Concentrate hot brothers:
make an angel of the snow
and shovel Sachsenhausen
silence from one side to the other
and back again.

O warmer Bruder
tonight you fall

shaping car windows
with triangles of Grangemouth light.
Smoke, the ghost of blood,
fills up the melting sky.

III

Blood dropped on Sachsenhausen
snow was silenced,
shoveled out of history.
But here in Scotland
it does not melt

and cloaks the Grangemouth
sky with red triangles.
This is no sunset
but concentrated smoke
that stings the eye.

IV

Triangles of smoke
blood the Grangemouth skies.
Along the Forth the hospice
workers shovel snow

from drives that keep the patients
bound, while silence, like an angel,
visits and stays on.

THREE WEE FREES

I   HINNIE-PIGS
   (or wan wee free)

thur wiz this wee free rite
an hi wiz doazin aff in a pew
wi the meenister goan on'n'on

sittin oan hiz hauns hi wiz
jist like at school when he pleyed
hinnie-pigs. Hinnie-pigs

wiz when wan o the boys
tried tae lift ye up by thi
oxters an gave ye three shakes

if yer hauns went aw flabby-like
ye wur a rite wersh wee git
an a bent shot intae the bargain!

a woofter man! If yer hauns
steyed pit ye wur a hinnie-pot or
pig an *youz* got a shot at the liftin.

wull. thur wiz this wee free rite
sittin tite oan his hauns
skretchin his erse as he snoozed

dreemin o hinnie-pigs when
all o a sudden its Jeezusiz' turn.
aye Jeezus! Christ! He sees Jeezus

dayin sum liftin. Jeezus the hinnie-
merchant feelin fur sweet oxters an
sour yins. wull blow me if he didni

chooz the biggest harry hoof
o the lot! am tellin ye hiz hauns
wur everywher, bloody whirligig he wiz.

an the wee free wiz fair gobsmacked
when he jalouzed that the guy doin
the jack'n'thi boax wiz the wee free

hisel an Jeezus seyin tae him: it's yoor
turn noo son. it's the nippy sweetie's turn.

II   LOT
                  (or anither wee free)

thur wiz this wee free rite
name o Lot wi a wifie missus Lot
an two braw lassies

steyed up a close in the Drum
pure mental they wur
tell ye why: wan day

Lot wiz haen a hingie
jist back fae the broo
the missus layin it aff

tae him aboot this an that
when all o a sudden he sees
angels o the lord

daunerin doon the road
wi a bunch o buggers
gien em the glad eye.

oot pops Lot an gobsmacks
the hail shabang: disnae
stoap tae ask hisel if the fowk

are angels an buggers
or which is which
but bundles the wans wi wings

up the close an offers
his weans tae the ithers
heavenly logic eh? weel

the buggers didny hae time
tae get ower the shock cause
Lot wiz oot wi a chain-saw

two minutes eftir. he got
Bar-L an the missus wiz turned
tae a pillar o salt.

III   THREE WEE FREES

thur wiz this wee free rite
doon in Glesca fur a day
at the virtual reality shoap

asks fur a new testament
vizor an turns up romans
1, 27: ye ken the bit aboot

men dayin 'shamefu things' wi ither
men. Paul caas em 'bangsters',
'scorners', 'sleekie' an 'ill-hairtit'

an the wee free wiz expectin
a bit o stonin at the verra least
men o God pittin oot sum een

when all o a sudden whit duz he see
but Davie an Eric oan their knees
afore the lord hisel hauns joined

thegither makin vows. aye. an the
Christ Jeezus blessin an smilin
sayin: 'lat him at hes lugs in his

heid hairken'. black affrontit
the wee free wiz. complained
tae the mainiger an goat his

reddies back: thirty pieces o siller.

from 'NEEDLEPOINT'

APARINE

Aparine siue Philanthropus, siue Omphacocarpos is called in English goosegrasse or Goosehareth, in Duche Klebkraute, in frenche Grateron, the herbe scoureth away and dryeth.

In June 1981, the Centers for Disease Control in Atlanta, Georgia receives its first reports of a relatively rare form of pneumonia, pneumocystis carinii pneumonia (PCP) and of outbreaks of Kaposi's sarcoma in young men. PCP was common amongst those liberated from concentration camps in Europe at the end of the Second World War.

BARBARE HERBA

Barbare herba groweth aboute Brokes and water sydes. It hath leaues lyke Rocket, wherefore it maye be called in Englishe wound-rocket for it is good for a wounde. Some cal thys Carpentarium.

NEEDLEPOINT

Injecting your name
through this soft quilt
with thread as red as blood,
I remember my domestic science grades
and stop.

I try to pass you through the eye
but everything dissolves in water.

Just as everything is free:
I can give you moons or oranges.
The words you kept up like spinning plates,
reinvent your signature.
Who will know but me.

Now my jongleur is in stitches
on this tapestry
and it is your smile
I wrap up in this flag.

It covers green fields when unfolded,
its nations visited by grieving
elderly in golf buggies and on bicycles,
a thing of shreds and patches,
moveable Passchendaele.

Yet I'm scared that in the night
I'll stretch out beneath my quilt
and will not find you among the names,
and turn to others, tongue-tied,
who travel further every year
seeking their own small country.

CYTISUS

Cytisus groweth plentuously in mount Appennine, I haue had it growyng in my gardine in high Germany, I haue not sene it in Englande. Cytisus may be called in Englishe tretrifoly.

THE DAY OF SAINT COLUMBA
adapted from Alexander Carmichael

Thursday of Saint Columba benign
Day to draw up the sheet upon his face
Day to zip up the green body-bag
Day to disinfect his bed.

Day to discard my plastic gloves
Day to collect his personal effects
Day to return the oxygen mask
Day to sleep and sleep

Day to converse with florists
Day to phone friends
Day of my beloved, the Thursday
Day of my beloved, the Thursday

The main structural constituents of HIV are:

— core proteins, derived from the Gag gene, which form the main internal structure of the virus. The most widely studied of these is known as p24.

— envelope glycoproteins, derived from the env gene, which cover the surface of the virus and play an important role in the interaction between virus and host cell. HIV envelope glycoproteins known as gp160, gp120 and gp41 also appear on the surface of infected cells and may therefore play a role in the spread of infection from cell to cell and in disease development.

— enzymes derived from the pol gene which catalyse a number of biochemical reactions in the virus life-cycle. The known enzymes are reverse transscriptase (RT), protease, endonuclease and ribonuclease H; all are possible targets for anti-viral drugs. In addition, there are a number of small proteins known as regulatory proteins which play a role in controlling and coordinating the events of the virus life cycle. These are derived from genes with code names such as TAT, REV, VIF, NEF.

NAMES

Now a kind of flesh is given back
to names which wasted, to all the signs
of life in Bernard, Tom, in Kurt and David:
four dogs, a kite, balloons, some last words stitched

in bubbles imprint their shapes on damp October
grass: we watch them soak in Washington dew.
At sunset, the quilt is thrown back
and tied in bales; the earth shows up a skein

of patches as if wild deer had pressed it
into sleep. Again we kneel and run
our fingers over still warm squares:
our short-term sons have just stepped out beyond

the field of vision and may be called to
among the dark paths of White House lawns.

Fragraria is called in English a strawbery leafe, whose fruite is called in englishe a strawbery, in duche Erdeber, in frenche Fraysne. Euery man knoweth wel inough where strawberies growe.

The sythesis of the HIV *proteins and consequent production of viral particles is controlled by a region of the* HIV *genome known as the long terminal repeat (*LTR*). Much effort by many laboratories, has therefore focused on factors which might influence activity of the* LTR.

A CHEVAL

The endless small light of the ward
spooled out his breath and breath:

a reeling, a casting off, taught thread
relaxed and then convulsively pulled
in to your smart finger;

a remembering, a forgetting, the clock's
calm bobbin pulling you around
its wooden grumbling centre

saying: safe now, a new pattern
sews in the fabric as easily
as the flowers your fingers grow for him.

Until the tearing anger unwinds itself
because it is all stitched, all sewn up.

You prick your finger
sleep for a hundred years
wake up, older by one square foot.

LITTLE QUAKING GRASS

Here then is my finger lullaby
pushing gently and withdrawing,
dolphining upon this quilt,
the trough and wave of cotton.

I hem your red boat with borders
and watch you sail on Washington grass,
whipping a green wake beneath you.

At dusk the park attendants rake
out your ocean: dandelions,
the usual chains of memory,
but also unexpected herbs

in all the languages we loved:
showy clover for my dustie-fute,
Kleines liebesgras,
Love-lies-bleeding,
and Live-forever,
Kleines zittergras.

GOSSIPIUM

Gossipium is called of Barbarus wryters, Bombax and Cononum, in englishe Coton, in greeke Pylon, in duche Baumewoll, in frenche ducotton. I never sawe it growyng sauing onely in Bonony.

LOVE CHARM
adapted from Alexander Carmichael

I took the foxglove
and the butterbur
to the broad flat flag

and sowed them in your silk

I cut nine stems of ferns
I took three lucky bones
from an old man's grave

and stitched them in your silk

I held your patch of quilt
against the morning light

against the sting of the north wind

And I will pledge and warrant you
this man will never leave you

YOU THREAD A SEA WITH YOUR EYE

Each time the needle enters your flank
the pain composes you;

trees that hung your voice
among their patterns
wrap your quilt in foliage;

a dog barks through the branches;
a girl's arm passes like an oar
across the sunlit patches;

now your song kneels
at the river's edge
and will not flow;

your passport head in pinned in silk.

A VISION OF W.S. GRAHAM'S HIPPOPOTAMUS IN VENICE

Each word is but a longing
        Set out to break from a difficult home.
        W.S. Graham, 'The Nightfishing'

What Graham heard first
was the matronly chafe
of her widow udders
on the Algonquin Hotel's
thick pile; what he saw

was the swing and the
prance of her all-
belly, softer and more velvet
than the empty, numbered
corridor; what he sent,

swimming across Iapetus,
was this old sea-cow
now wellingtoned
in Venetian shallows
as real as yellow
café chairs rafting
marble and meltwater.

Hippo moons at Byzantine
domes seeking us
out of the crowd.
And I pray that – gingerly –
she'll not step up
onto duckboards
and mince our way...

But she does
and the city sinks at last.

I am lagooned in silence
until the lapping torches
nuzzling Palazzi stairs dive
down like bell anemone
and phosphoresce the green.

And then through the flood
I hear the slightly panicked
whirr of castagnetting hippo
feet as they lose their grip
and power churn the water-burn

down to me: her skirts of flesh
bulge out, her piggy blue
mosaic eyes and Pantactrator
face, benevolent as Mary
Poppins, peer out at me.

She seems to speak
a delicate fossil tongue
and tells me it's the one
will buoy me up again
and recreate the stones of Venice.

So we dredge the sludge
of Istrian effluent, dodge
drowning ducal piles
and make our treasure-chest
discovery beneath the cemetery isle:

a cache of language
beneath the Fondamenta,
waterlogged parchments
of Scottish glossaries
plugging the solid caranto;

here is a dull broach of
lion drenched in a
summer-sob, there a
map of *water-gaw*
where it all began again.

But her hooves crunch over
the coralled etymologies:
runined horny grapolites
that only once caught sense
in tiny comb-like sieves.

Here is a stash of *utteridge*
strewn and *unmensefu*,
the *undersook*
of 'Sestieri': a *sumphie*
stour-o-words.

There is *maroonjous* pine
that Gritti and Ca Rezonnico
deliquesce upon, the water-
slain-moss that peats their roots
and eats their damp-proof stone.

Oh for a *neid-fire*
to ignite canals
electrify a doge of sound
that would convoke
the glittering, *dowie* signifiers.

I turn in the *wallowa*,
turn to hippo in the *wallowae*,
but she's slipped aloft already,
a 'cathédrale engloutie'
burbling on her mobile.

I wonder in the *howe-dumb-deid*
beneath the 'canalazzo'
wonder at that hoof
of *umbersorrow* lit
by the lagoon's blue day,
wonder what my hippo
is using me for.

Glossary

Summer-sob — frequent light rains in summer; *water-gaw* —
the fragment of a rainbow appearing in the horizon; seen in
the north or east, a sign of bad weather; *utteridge* — utterance,
power of speech; *unmensefu* — disorderly; unbecoming;
indiscreet; used of weather: rough, unseasonable; *undersook*
— an undercurrent flowing against that on the surface;
sumphie — stupid, foolish; sulky, sullen; *stour-o-words* — a
wordy discourse; *maroonjous* — harsh, sturdy; *neid-fire* — fire
produced from the friction of two pieces of wood; a beacon-
fire, also used to express the phosphoric light of rotten wood;
dowie — sad, mournful, inclined to decay; *wallowa / ae* —
an exclamation of sorrow, the devil; *howe-dumb-deid* — used
of night, the middle, when silence reigns; *umbersorrow* —
surliness, resisting disease or the effects of bad weather.

TO A BARDIE

fae a cockroach, on jumping out of a New York fridge and confronting him, July 1997

'The cockroaches like nuggets half hid in the bran',
Frank O'Hara, 'Alma'.

Huge, baldit, chitterin, timrous bardie,
Openin the fridge wiz richt fuhardie!
Weel micht ye fart awa ma lairdie
    Wi 'Christ, a cockroach!'
I wad jist luv tae rin an chase thee
    Wi murd'ring reproach!

Welcome tae ma sweltrin bothy,
This liftless scraper, clammy, growthie.
It cracks me up tae see you drouthy.
    Tough! Ahv drunk the beer,
Munched the bran O'Hara slipped sae poofy-
    Like in here.

Which pairts wad ye hae me play? James Dean?
Your frien fancied him enough, the lean
Cute, saft smoulder o his outcast een
    Jessie rebel!
Whit cause is worth a nicht i' mean
    Cockroach hotel?!

Aye right! Ma Bronx bodywork's a smash
In motion, ma brow a buckled dash
Board, twitchin, sniffin the stashed hash
    O ma guid cousin,
Hit n'run Gekko wi Groucho tache,
    Corlione's chin.

Or wad it be Ginger, wee Tom Cruise
Pas de deuxing wi Mel whose fuse
Is too short fur his kilt! You choose!
    Brief Encounter?
No brief enough fur me, sae muse
    On Lana Turner!

You'd like tae find a symbol in me:
N'this dreich hole ahm Cocteau's repartee,
Fleur du mal sookin up the ennui
    O bein you,
Core o the Big Aipple's bel esprit.
    Twad mak me spew!

Frank grew oot o this an aw the folk
He toasted wi his can o coke,
Grace, Patsy, Warren, Kenneth Koch
    Suffered nae sea-change,
Risin fae Fire Island waves, soaked,
    Mair themsels, strange.

Jist a cockroach in a New York fridge
You've writ a poem tae, nae bridge
Tae sumfin bigger an masel, abridged
    Myth, camp and free.
You're the wan gaes on his nerve, on edge,
    In tongues, no me.

Glossary

Bothy — a makeshift hut; *growthie* — warm and moist;
drouthy — thirsty; *een* — eyes.

WALL

PYRAMUS: O, kiss me through the hole of this vile wall!
THISBE: I kiss the wall's hole, not your lips at all.
              Shakespeare, *A Midsummer Night's Dream*

Look at the wall, the sweet and lovely
wall we carry with us in public places.
Even in meadows when we rest it
for a second on muscular buttercups,

its tinyness glimpsed from the distances
of outer galaxies is not as small
as the monstrous little voice
I use to whisper to you through its chink.

And in the streets of Glasgow
where we set it down despite the looks
to share affection over *lattes* and Versace suits
we can hear the awkward avalanche

of lime and mortar evolve within its frame
as we kneel down and seek out
chink and speak our cherry words
knit up in hair and stone.

Even here on Pearblossom Highway
or Garrowby Hill where you can barely
see it for the Hockney colours
and sentimentalists mistake it for a rainbow

it is a wall that bears our mottoes of restraint.
And in the Japanese storyboard
of Chris and Don's Malibu interior
where even the wicker chairs are clearly

gay, at ease with their own maturity,
Wall balances between the pockets
of our cargo pants as we meander through,
fearful of prat-fall, putty on the pinewood floor.

Some say Chink offers us the virtue
of cubist perspective: the silk forest
of your ear-lobe's blonde still-baby
hairs. Polaroided and collaged

in a cakewalk of mismatching
edges, our groins grow a wall.
Exciting textures are described
but no-one ever asks us what it weighs.

Others tell us to ignore it, drape
our bodies in a magnetic web
of invisible embraces, a shimmering
virtual cloth of Proustain complexity

beyond the deconstructive powers
of Peter Quince. We touch our asses
heads like caps, pick up our wall
and walk. True, Chink's lynx eye

offers us a precious parsimony
of moments: the time the slits
of our lapels smiled to fill the whole
of that slim orifice, the time

your pinkie stroked a whisker
of my orange tawny beard,
my purple-in-grain beard,
my French crown-colour beard!

And no-one noticed!
But those who see our wall and label it
know about its chink as well,
the slight pucker of its lips

which taste of cold chipped tile,
name it only for the fuck-hole
of Bully Bottom's rude mechanicals.
Everywhere we turn we find out

moonshine. Smash wall!
Smash the person of wall
and the person
of pure moonshine!

THE BARRIER

But good-night! — God bless-you!
    The stillness of true loss:
Sterne says that is equal to a kiss:
    it wakes with him. It is
yet I would rather give you the kiss
    the moment before full
into the bargain, glowing with
    consciousness and the
gratitude to heaven, and affection
    moment after. It is the
to you. I like the word affection,
    utter stillness of pure
because it signifies something
    loss held like a sweet
habitual; and we seem to
    contemplated face in the
meet, to try whether we have
    bed of love, held for a
mind enough to keep our
    second before movement,
hearts warm. — Mary.
    before life. It is the descending
I will be at the barrier
    certainty that you are purely
a little after ten o'clock,
    alone forever and that no one,
tomorrow.
    no one can ever touch that

loneliness and loss.
Mary Wollstonecraft

Turned away from me,

I read the sadness of pure
loss as it floods his face –
although I cannot see it.
The still terror and yet
the acceptance of that
terror in the silent morning
bed before light and
movement. The impossibility
of fully naming it, the im-
possibility of being in it.

BED

The moment the light goes out,
he sleeps: a gift from the dark.
There is the small chime
of the moon on the wall,
the deep freeze digesting
in the kitchen. He floats
from head to toe on the buzz
of his snore, dreaming the calm
glide of a Jasper ski-lift,
the summer elk that trotted
out of forest beneath our
dangling feet. His arm
crooks the violin of my head.
I elbow him away intent on
sleep but suddenly unpegged
by a gust of dreams we roll
together in the hot hole
of his mum's old bed,
dribbling on the pillows.
Waking, he has me in an
arm-lock, our legs a single
rope of flesh, my ear-lobe
tickled by his breath. I reach
behind me and shove my hand
between his thighs. He stretches,
opening briefly like a centre-
fold, a light smile of welcome
on his lips. But more than this
is the scrape of the two-o'clock

beetle, the nip of a dust-mite,
my scratch: my love disturbed
by me, awake but patient
in the dark.

FIFTH QUARTER

i.m. Derek Jarman

INVOCATION

Ariel, 'pearl of fire',
clarified spirit —
(There is a mouseguard
on the beehive,
safe: all
golden things) —
doodle, Ariel,
inhumane, distracted,
blood shingle by the shore
for water-courses
and shower us:
Derek in a wizard's hat
spelling Dungeness sands.

SUPER 8

In his childhood's manuscript,
sparkles flowered: 'I remember
daisies, words like *Zuassa*
and *Maggiore* that would not
stiffen, even at the scent of lime.'

Like a crow you stole
all cinema's glistening
detritus, hiding the tea-spoons,
the clothes-pegs,
the baking foil,
pinning them to the santolina,

the helidrysum of the screen
which chirrups at us
like a silver jubilee.

Light banks
the cascades
are quite worn through

STILL

O bee-hat
above a shepherd's crook
herding pebbles
into wiriness

CROSSFADE

to the solve of flood: a water hand, a sensitive hand churns
in the waves. His palms kindle foam, an alchemy of bubbles,
seeking soap stone, tearing with the roman vitriol of nails.
Lightening palm, palm the colour of honey, white arsenic.
Look! The serpent life-line, *originall of Nilus*, changes the
sea into itself, its smoky blue, its seeded white, a finer bone, a
fist of rivered veins. A man of vinegar is being born, of slow
heat, quicklime, retort and potash. Saltpetre hand, hand of
cinnebar and verdigris seeking the sun, here no there no it's
water no air no light no flame no it's the flower it's blue it's
blue it's blue

From the sand
The gentle man
From the shell
The gentle boy
In cardigan
And Calvin Kleins
Breasting the surf
With down and tan
Beneath the sodden
Wool and cotton

His footprint warms
The winter beach
The grains beneath
The balls of feet
Swell slightly
To caress his
Firm instep

Ferdinand always
Ferdinand even
In the combat gear
Of shipwreck
Hair in place
Despite the tempest
A strapping pet
Waterlogged but snoggable
Making for the dunes

STILLS

Still speeding lens
Net against chest
Rope against
Chords of muscle

Windchimes   A verdigris trumpet

A dwarf pear

ER ... A TEMPEST

'OK! ACTION! Right, whattawegot?' 'Shipwreck. Multiple
facial abrasion, scalp lacerations, penetrating trauma to zone
two of the neck. One ... er ... Caliban. No first name. BPs 98
over 60, pulse 92, reps 24. Moon calf floored by a thunder-
stroke. No guarding or rebound tenderness, normal ball
sounds. Log roll him. One, two, three! Admit axelary line.'
'Watyaseekid? Whatyasee? Pan in, pan in!' 'His arms betrims
and thatch of meads, his stover sullied, liver trampled by live
nibbling sheep, a gut of wheat, rye, barley, vetches, oats and
pease but half-digested, traces of pyroxidine, carbamazepine,
tracking through that watry arch now, formed by rib cage.
Yes! A grass plot. There peacocks fly amain. I'm framing up
his bosky acres and his uncrushed down. Amazing! What
a montage! His spongy April is completely overgrown by
broom-groves. This is one heck of a dismissèd bachelor! Focus
on that waspish head embedded in his abdomen. Death was
no honey-drop, soured refreshings, scandalled company! Poor
guy! Have you ever seen such a blue bow, saffron wings, rich
scarf, such a Caliban?

STILLS

Escaped periwinkle   Sulphudiazine   Laceflower

And Ariel of course
Is a little trowel
Who'll hatch
From the gentle
Bunch of Barry's
Forearm as he lifts
Fags from the corners
Of his mouth: for you
For me

SHORT

Dark slowly maps
The salt-sea marsh

Wave flows to wave;
Sunglut; a shell
Gloops and light
Is born through
A shinglequake

This is the fifth
Quarter of the globe
All outside is here
And he is at home

Glitters a dull pewter
His hair

PROSPECT

nuff said

here: the reindeer moss

imagine   its dapples

… nuff heard

dodder or

muted rainbow

At every air
You are fenceless

och … nuff

Rest-harrow
Beautiful and necessary
weed

Note: Derek Jarman, the British film director, died of AIDS in 1994. His films include *Jubilee, The Last of England, Caravaggio* and adaptations of Shakespeare's *The Tempest* and Marlowe's *Edward II*. During the final years of his life, he came to live in Prospect Cottage on the south coast of England near the Dungeness Power Station and created a remarkable garden out of this bleak, beautiful landscape. It is celebrated in his film *The Garden*.

from *In My Father's House* (2005)

I PRESUME

In this opera, my Dad is Doctor
Livingstone lost in inclement bush
and I am Stanley trying to think
what I will say to him across the rapids
of our handshake.

It is Act 3: a bank of krieg lights
blanch unstinted draughts of a water-hole
putrid with the stage-designer's
vision of rhinoceros dung.

I am in the pit of doubt
unwinding a recitative:
'Commit thy way unto the Lord
and he shall direct thy steps.'
I stumble on the phrase:

'Is this all gammon?'
and on cue my head turns
back: 'Doctor Living
stone, I presume':
a statement of his presence.

He seems to die before me:
unaccompanied, he crumples
on the sedgy grass but then
the hell of music takes him
for the Don he is;

bramble papyrus thick as a wrist
wraps about his feet as he
arpeggios down like hippos
of the flooded valleys,
entering embezzled 'discoveries',

the humid theatre of his past
where he arranged 'beyond
every other man's line of things'
ritornellos of rivers,

navigable highways to arias
of liveable plateaux: fantasies
of a fake missionary
and missionary 'murderer!'

I presume your family craved an ending
to the hundred and seventy-six
verse psalms of greasepaint
rife with prodigious ticks and lice,
recognition that the tales of

falls were true. I presume
your son devoutly wished
God's song would stop:
it finally did

and in the darkness
emanating from the flies
we discover a silence
at the heart of music
even in the silent stave.

I sleep upon one note of hope;
that brief strain —
was it prologue or flashbacked
epilogue? — those tears
when you dropped your oatcake
in the burn at Hamilton.

TREMMLIN TREE

eftir the German o Paul Celan

Tremmlin tree, your leaves blink white intae daurk
Ma mither's hair wiz nivver white.

Dainty-lion, so green is the Ukraine,
Ma lint-white mither didnae come hame.

Rain clud, dae ye swither at the well?
Ma lown mither greets for all.

Roondit stern ye rowe the gowden loop
Ma mither's hert wiz hurt by lead.

Aiken door, wha hoised ye aff yer hinges
Ma douce mither cannae come back.

Tremmlin tree — aspen; *dainty-lion* — dandelion; *lint-white*
— white as flax, flaxen blond; *clud* — cloud; *swither* — be
uncertain, move fitfully; *lown* — quiet, subdued; *greet* — weep;
rowe — roll, coil; *Aiken* — oaken; *hoised* — raised, hoisted;
douce — gentle.

AN ENCOUNTER

In Cardross Cemetery:
'Iain Crichton Smith';

a poet so alive to death
it made him real at last.

Four rows down —
my father — Dad.

In this little theatre
of words I make for them,

my Dad, who sold his kingdom
for booze and metaphor,

keeping death's whinny
far down the neighbour's field,

steps out of character and passes
swiftly through the audience of midnight stones,

fleeing from this real dead poet
as if he'd seen a ghost.

REMISSION

for Gerry McGrath

The rash of russet earth.
Strewn. For remission.

In the Autumn
remission came for him,

folded back the cancer
and he seized the Winter

space it left him, filled
it with his fruits, his songs

and in the glacial energy
of love borrowed from death

we were born. Then, he seemed
the place in which the immaculate

distant pines met their reflection:
the sure clasp of earth itself,

a steady ground that could not end.
After a fairy tale that took him

twenty years to tell, the birches
shivered out their silver

and Spring and Summer came back
with his delayed remittance.

BAINES HIS DISSECTION

for Donny O'Rourke

1.   A PROCESSION

For hours now: a little scraping tear,
scratchings, a dab, a blot; then it runs
again – blue, red – coagulates tired
eyes, swims in tears: the quill tears up
the grain of paper, reflecting it away
like skin, finger-forceps grip tense
the flap, scalp through deep fascia
to the muscles of sense.
That scrape again. Is it me
or the witter of the small barboni fish
hung from cabin beams whose thin blue light
dries out like rotten wood?
The parchment heaves up
with its choppy words once sheathed
in the fibrous tunic of a Medway oak,
white, fusiform, cleaned, defined,
dissected into compass timber or stretched
tight for sea or study scroll. Beneath bark
this paper vessel ran like ink or blood,
its sap beating in tendons for the coffin
of my friend, Sir Thomas Baines, embalmed in brandy.
He floats next door. Not door. No. Mere canvas,
an indoor sail, still unless moved
by my erratic breath. His trestle glimmers,
looms in the palimpsest of candle-light,
trembles in the harbour's toy troughs and crests.
He spurned play but it got him at the last:
the Ambassador's companion borne in pomp

by twenty-six bostancis, muftis, imams, kadis,
down from Pera, Galatea, wreathed in salutes
of gun-smoke. A cenotaph stood for three days
in the Captain's cabin, covered with a pall,
a sabred dervish by his scutcheon (sable
two bones crosswise argent), six great tapers
burning by in six great silver candlesticks.
'*Monsu arrivar!*' The pidgin Italian of the Turks!
That off-hand, intimate, distant, haughty race,
cruel and playful, obsessed with ceremony,
stopping trade to make fine shows of it
while eleven thousand boys had their prepuces
cut off at the Crown Prince's circumcision.
We witnessed that procession: wagon
upon wagon each with its nesting guild,
shoemakers, tailors, weavers, all set out
with tokens of their art, bakers kneading loaves
the size of hammam domes, smiths stoking
little forges and walking gardens full of flowers
with waxwork fruits held in slings by slaves.
As they kicked up a perfect Egyptian mist of dust
you stood beside me, Tom, and called it
'hobbyhorsism folly!' Silenced by the fireworks battle
though, the Seraglio lit up in a thousand
camphor balls of pure white fire.
Fire, procession, ceremony.
There's something to be said for it
and I'm determined we'll have our own display,
dear Tom, our profession of unusual friendship,
our trade as doctors, diplomats, decked out
upon a Cambridge tomb, our ensigns of affection
flagged up and out for prayerful and tourist to decipher.
Embalmed within that stone or living our spiritual life
like the ghosts of holy Turks beside their kiosks,

we'll move as we have always done in one harmonious
cavalcade, two bodies, one soul, the craft of love.
Except there is for now one person less
and I, John Finch, Ambassador to the Porte,
am less in consequence; 'Dosti!', 'Dear Friend!'
'Aman!' 'Janum!' 'Mercy!' 'My Soul!' 'Kuzum!'
'My Lamb!', unsteadily I grip your coffin's berth
and look through a glass to your face below,
spirits of wine preserve its peaceful countenance
and momentarily it swells beneath my gaze
as if caught up in drops of oil spat out
by divers to magnify the minute objects of the deep.
My spirit diver, swim beside me on our voyage
home, protect me from storm and mermaid
and the ebb and flow of memory.

2.   AN ANATOMY

We are goat born, my Baines,
like Marsyas, fit only to be flayed,
little worlds of inner secrets
split by the lynx-like knife.
In Padua and Pisa I got those skills
which I can turn on you in intimacies
of autopsy without a flinch: my love,
my work now perfectly combined.
Our Muslim surgeons could not oblige
and so I incise and cut, scour
brain and abdomen, aspirate gases
with a trocar. Where the heart beat
I place musk, sweet-basil in the kidney-bed,
quince in ala of the sacrum.

Saffron, violets, ambergris attack bacteria.
I repack the skull with honey.
Spooning in Constantinople moonlight
just a month before the end
I noticed how your nape grew dark hairs yet,
recalled how thirty-six years ago, snug
in the same view, I imagined how each one
would be white one day. It gave me hope.
'*Una mana con occhio!*' 'A hand with eyes!'
whose skill could kindle infinite desire
now excavates the bladder for stones
that led you to your tomb. Irony
and renal colic were the dead ends
of distorted crypts that burrowed out
the ureteric musculature.
How you strained to void those philosophic calculi,
another joke that made you smile through pain.
And yet those phosphate stones
had serious facets too: 'Lapis est,
quem Salomonis architecti rejecerunt.'
What niche for us in the Temple
of King Solomon's England?
And so we rolled in exile across Europe,
gathering the moss of learning, liberty, love.
Royal servants, yes, but at a distance.
I stone the body of my lover, eviscerate
and then the glorious mineral
in three days reconstitutes itself.
As cousin Harvey's good friend Donne once wrote:
'He was all gold when he lay
down but rose all tincture!'
Oh, Tom! The alchemists have myriad names for you:
body of magnesia, the light of lights,
marvellous father, fugitive servant.

You are rubine stone and chaos,
toad, green lion, virgin's milk.
You are Brazil! Or simply 'Fava'
as our Italians called you, hearing 'bean' for Baines!
No matter! But that's not *quite* the point:
matter *and* spirit, spirit *in* matter
to conjure until it effervesces
like the semen which seems contagious
for Harvey found no trace of it
within the ovum after sex.
How else explain the love of like for like
as well as different? Our Cambridge tutors
had the gist of it before modern science
got there too. They flew above the high and airy
hills of Platonism, disdained democritism
which so embases and enthralls.
More and Cudworth, good men who studied
to spiritualise their bodies not to incarnate
their souls, who thought Heaven first a temper,
then a place. In his enthusiastic middle age,
More shook like a Quaker in the threshold
of his body, tasting distinctions
in the cabalistic weather as our ship's captain
tries the *imbat* which will carry us to sea.
That warm wind proves, to paraphrase Ficino,
that spirit is a very subtle body, almost soul,
not a soul and almost body. So, bent upon
this clotted and compacted corpse
I pare away the veins, capillaries and arteries,
reveal that luciform and attenuate vehicle,
transparent stone stuck in my balm of unguents.
Poor Baines, caught in a coat of resin
and pinned within a tree!
We are like tortoises in the Age of Tulips:

we strap small lamps upon our backs
and creep among the parterres of the night
so the distant think we are light itself
or tulips strolling among tulips.
Suspended disbelief! The tortoises
circle lamplight endlessly among the Gardens
of Felicity, small ventricles of light slowly
pulsing through the tulip fields as blood
pumps out to the periphery and then returns,
preserved. Yet cousin Harvey acknowledged
with *Leviticus* that the blood is soul,
numinous *and* turgescent, matter *and* force
as long as it moves in vessels: *cor a currendo*,
not this sorry *cruor*, this gore
I mop from the dissection table.
And so we moved continuously, sharing *mot*
et motion. When coaches failed we hired sedans
and grew a self so interpersonal each could say
'I think, therefore, we are,' wherever
the Red Apple of dominion settled
we were Zeno's arrow, shaft and quiver,
barely different, presenting motion
and then decamping. Out. Elsewhere.

3.   DALLAM'S FANTASY

I return to Cambridge on the Oxford.
Spires shuffle in my memory, changeable
as the very spindle of the main top mast
or wamblings of my stomach which shears
off according to the emotions of the Euripus.
I sip a little sack and wormwood to calm
the humours, but England, the world even,

a poet may someday say is as variable
as the *Euripus*. It waxes, wanes with ages
of the moon. When we first loved each other
it seemed to be an isle of bells, debate
and woodsmoke wafting over playing fields,
annealed to the Universe by amber cupolas.
A steady place. And so it was. But steadiness
runs deep and from the depths our masters
looked at us and seeing chaos
where only difference lurked or a surfeit of similitude
suggested silence or torture for sedition.
We linked hands and left. First Paris
where I rejoiced to see old Calvin's house
reduced to a dunghill, fit epitaph
for the man who burnt Servetus on a pyre
for proposing the lesser circulation
of the blood. And then our tour of Italy
which lasted twenty-two good years:
we made Pro-Rector, Syndic of Padua University,
Resident at Florence to the Grand Duke of Tuscany;
Ambassador, we learned to deal in trade capitulations
while great physicians of the day,
Malphighi, Borelli, Fracassati, Truttwyn
called us friends. When we went home
it was to be knighted, doctors to the Queen.
But in between it was as if our country also left:
one king lost his head, a farmer ruled,
around 1650 some folk noticed, really noticed
America was there and that the moon
and other planets perhaps existed for themselves
and not for us. New ways of praying
flak the air like volleys of small shot
and in the dim, dank lanes of London wynds
they open places for 'our kind'. 'Our kind'!
The fact that I can say this is the point.

And others say it too and persecute *and* tolerate.
We did not like this either and so we left again.
Plurality does not concern the Turks.
Severe but subtle they denote rank by perfume,
are not afraid if the religions of their Empire mingle too.
Nationality is a career 'and not a cause'.
Beauty not gender is seductive.
When passion left us, I was lonely
and now I face the final loneliness.
But then we discovered, together and separately,
the bow-like eyebrows of tall Persians,
how good Armenians or silver-chested Greeks
feel against the cold, that Baghdad boys
like torturing 'and never keep appointments'.*
So the flavour of our happiness had gradations
that would surprise a superintendent of fine sherbets.
Not *being* but *coming into being* was our forte.
Seamen, semen, pneumatic blood concurred.
Even plague whose venomous and sticky atoms
took up abode in miasmatic air and chased us
from the city to a town of tents and back again.
And yet, and *so* I cannot stay. For even
'the Refuge of the World' has blind spots.
I cannot live well in a city crawling with calligraphy,
weltering in words that banish even as they gesture
in and to the stones they're written on. Nothing
can be left to contemplation, the partially
uninstructed stare. No pictures here then,
no simulacra of the human, little music
which is a spirit like our own. How the ship's bells
peel me back to Cambridge from the drone of muezzin!
Another shape wavers through the canvas
by my Baines' coffin, it too a wrack of organs:
Dallam's mechanical fantasy,

a gift from old Queen Bess to some forgotten Sultan,
is now sent back 'to be repaired', in fact
is banished for its display of personages
which stands at two corners of the second storey,
lift trumpets to their heads and sound a tantarra.
In better times this organ played a song of five parts
twice over and on the casement top did sit
a holly bush full of blackbirds and thrushes
which at the music's end sang and shook their wings.
Why did it offend so much? When Baines
had audience with the Vani Effendi he was told
the Blessed went not into Paradise
until the Day of Judgement but had continual
sight of it through one great window.
Perhaps he sees it from his little porthole now.
Is the principle not the same? We veer
predictably, our tack on the divine
is rude and artificial. We stand on tip-toe
at a threshold or a casement and then are flung
upon the cabin floor made giddy by our reach
and lack of it. But after the Marmarean sunset,
the gentle jangling of that instrument,
as the ship slides over into sleep,
stirs my blood like tulip-wine and I hear my lover
slip his veins of oak and colonise the organ
moving it ineffably. Then he sees and seizes me
in sound, his eyes, two knarled cherry plugs
of song, rush forth on tiny thrushes wings
like butterflies of soul. His hair enwreathes
the cabin with arias that wake the sap
in coffined wood and crescendo on a note
so pure it dissects me as I shiver
in my hammock's pitch. The air becomes
a partial gauze: minims, quavers, blackbirds

stick to its interstices, waft a web
of tenor chirrups which then break off,
float down, a snow of feathered trills
that deliquesce upon my skin, vibrate
the tissues until all the vessels
of this little world are cloaked and magnified
in tune, a music that is his, is mine, is Dallam's
and all the spirits that transport us.

*NOTE: Among the texts on which I have drawn here I
wish to acknowledge particularly the work of Philip Mansel,
whose wonderful book *Constantinople: City of the World's
Desire, 1453–1924* (Penguin, 1997) was a source of much
inspiration. This description of the Armenians, Greeks and
Baghdad boys is indebted to his transcription of details
taken from Fazil Bey's (1759–1810) *Khubanname* (The Book
of Beauties). Bey's dates are of course later than those of
Finch and Baines, but I hope the reader may allow me this
licence on the grounds that the same pleasures were possibly
available during this earlier period.

The 'Red Apple' was a Turkish phrase for whichever city was
considered to form the capital of the known world.

MARY STUART'S DREAM

Reine de France Marie, 'Quatrain', Mary, Queen of Scots

When I sit late at works, almost
within the verdure of this tower's
only tapestry — rabbits in an orange tree
by my shoulder — an old globe
chases silly latitudes beneath
the casement window and, looking out,
the scant, dank countryside makes up
fields of Poitou mist. Distantly at first,
— but the globe birls it closer— a giant
oak shaped like a country crests
towards my berth. A man wreathed
in raindrops disembarks. Do the King's
swans flee him? Is that cry a peacock
at midday? I hear his feet discretely
pad the pockmarked steps and now
he is before me. Alone. With his box
of little instruments. He is a humble man
and the Scots leid on his lips is just
the burr that made my cradle sleepy.
Together we compare our cabinet of works:
my *petit point*, his burin, my panels
of darned net, his tiny hammers,
chalk and chisels, a balletic compass
to take the measure of my smile.
I laugh and show him coins a plenty:
billons, testoons emblazoned with my features
and the King's, French treasure of our large
estates and mottos, trees of Jesse, crosses,
fleurs de lys and lion rampant. Poor man!

His journey has been fruitless. And yet
he shields his eyes against my two poor
candles and beckons me down the cold
stone steps towards his ship quoting
Leonardo: 'In the streets at twilight, Madam,
note the faces of men and women
when the weather is bad, how much attractiveness
is seen in them.' He will draw me,
draw me into the haar which lies on
this strange country like a mourning veil.
I nod above my embroidery, start awake
and hunt for my jewelled casket,
feverishly fingering small change
for the evidence of my head.

A COIN

for Edwin Morgan

John Acheson struck me. Master of the Mint,
he was engraver to the Medicis and the Scottish queen
whose portrait he dug hard for in my golden flesh.
His hands twisted out the corkscrew curls,
scraped the swan-like neck for heads,
lion rampants for my tails. I've aged with her,
my high colour burnished, though still
I offer her an image of her profile on the brink
of greatness: Great Queen of France and Scots
and England, her crown both regal and the tiara
of her Roman faith. Tip me to certain angles
in the sunlight and you'll catch reflections
of Chambord afternoons and at night a glimmer
of the candles ranked and raked on ballroom floors.
I announced a Golden Age and she has used me well
to pay off poets, artists, murderers
though each was just by proxy.
Her time twindles now but I am constant.
Save once: when someone threw me in a pond
of goldfish for good luck. I sank
and as the water's fingers stroked my rim,
the sacred profile that I carry wavered
in the shallows as if struck clumsily
in another age or country, peered
helplessly through weird vegetation,
mirk, mist, and for a moment I seemed to mark
a different story, crossed by dark shapes
I did not recognise. One of the Maries
fished me out, restored me to that brilliant reign.
Although to do so went against a powerful wish.

RESISTING HELL

i.m. Esther Inglis, calligrapher, 1571–1624

I

Victorious and venerable King, most virtuous scholar,
I, Esther Inglis, calligrapher, humbly send this tiny buik of
Valediction. My husband — who once spied for you — bears final
Envoi. It is written in a hand called Death and hails from

Leith, a town I etch within triangular serifs
And a trembling line. Its smoke curls up initial capitals, ignites

Preface, this epistle which crawls immaculately to you. High
Lord of Scots, of England, France; we both enjoy the tribute of our
Underlings: mine are these poems in my praise by Kinloch,
Melville, references stitched up in Latin and pasted in for
Esther, 'paragon and matchless mistress of the golden pen'.

II

Recovering the spirit of 'ane Amazon',
Esther stipples an oval ground of cobalt blue.
She seats herself in front of sheet music, quill and ink,
Inscribes her portraits complete with hats that say it all:
Some are smart and conical above a ruff, others low crowned
Thumb Bible sized, picked from the rack of emblemata that
Inventory her life: here are leeks and monkeys, tassels and white urns;
Naomi, Sarah, Rebecca; Susannah, Hannah, Judith: no lady in a
Garden could be as patient, meek and brave as this medicinable
Hand, slippered in long gloves, herb script of *lettre pattée*, of *lettera rognosa*,
Easing out the periods of her silent race, the pinks and pansies of shame-fas
Lord! Oh, my tottering right hand offers up one
Last velvet strawberry, this silky anagram:

I dreamt that I was at my escritoire again:
dawn over Leith and Leith nestling in the curling
terminals I give the letter C of Christ our Lord.
And then I dreamt the tiny town spoke from the hand
they call *civilité*, cried out to Esther crouched
with her crow quill over bees and whirlpool motifs.
I dreamt that little people clinging to the roofs
or snug in the crow's nest of a cresting ship
spied how my lines of *lettera mancina*
undulate eternally from page to page.
I saw the people balance dizzily
and drown in a kaleidoscope of shapes.
I dreamt they screamed that they were trapped
in language and lonely, wrecked in a partial view:
a few red tiles, a single sail and then I felt
my forty different hands weigh down
my body like nights of wilderness.
I dreamt this flattened costal town
was all that I could get of life,
just several strokes of *chancery*
beneath grotesques and river goddesses.
And that my art was copied from the books of men.

EDWIN MORGAN IS EATING AN ORANGE

Edwin Morgan is eating an orange.
'Tasty, zesty orange,' he mutters.

Edwin Morgan folds the segments back
and shrinks to the size of a pip.

Edwin Morgan cradles each piece of peel
in the small of his bony hand.

Edwin Morgan steps into the orange
and zips up the lithe behind him.

Edwin Morgan's taxi driver
and Edwin Morgan's interviewer
step into Edwin Morgan's room.

The journalist lurches off again,
mystified, disappointed,
and the taxi driver pockets an orange.

I, GIRAFFE

Sous le pont Mirabeau
coule la Seine – Apollinaire

I, Giraffe, *camelopardalis*,
once dappled, high on mimosa trees,
raft and dam this second flood:

they hammer feverishly beside me,
– Lilliputians with their guys and ropes –
tautening an ark against the ever rising Seine;
a dilute version of Gustave Eiffel's tower
emerges like Leviathan:
a scaffolding to save or break

my neck. Yesterday I lost sensation
in my feet but fret not for this heart
has pressure valves large enough
to lock down oceans of my blood.
Stand proud, my father said, *we may be lifers*
in a zoo but they have made a guddle
of this damp city and all the world beyond.

Once, he told me how we all began:
Giraffa of the order Artiodactyla
were trees that moved and got their spots
from strolling through the leaves
that left their shade on them.

He spoke of a creature called 'savannah',
rich in acacia and a delicious
whistling thorn; the resident oxpecker
which roamed his person like a daemon

for unwanted ticks, the black piapicks
that sieved the air for insects.

It has begun to stink. This morning
I spied a rat swim past my right hind leg.
Small fires dot the cityscape
and a man shuffles on two chairs
across the deluge. He says: *This is a street.*

There is no river here. And drowns.
A minute iceberg crowns his debris.

Now even the gas lighters have gone
and it is dark as the bush at sunset.
Paris is a city of pontoons and floating *passerelles*
and I nap uneasily as small punts prowl
the outskirts of our zoo. At 10 I woke
to see them float the hippopotamus away,
his rump bulbous in the moonlight.
Yet he could have swum!

Ghosts of my hunted ancestors haunt my dreams:
Baringos impressed for buttons, Rothschilds
reduced to thread and guitar strings,
the bladder of a Hock stitched for a water-bag.
Parisians! I am a simple reticulated camel-cow
and abjure aristocratic forbears.
I am not good to eat! Waterlogged and knobbly
I shiver as dawn floods the abandoned garden.

*

It is too late. My squire the donkey
makes final obeisance in a sympathetic
neigh: *Passe avant, sieur Sarapha!*

Move on now to the next world.
This earth is all unstitched
its colours washed away.

So I swing my head along the arc
of all my longing.
The rivers' waters move like wings about me,
the days thrash; my single leg
– icy, seraphically numb –
harrows this flood like a pestle.

I pass; I pass; the days remain,
rain-washed, hand in hand.
Rivers become the towers,
hooves of all the little people
bob among the eddies;
upended trees, dishevelled wigs
root among the waves.

Doused hopefulness
of this long, slow life;
love comes and goes
and goes; the days remain.

ARROW MEN

after a magazine illustration by J.C. Leyendecker

All I can see of Joe's face lost
behind the paper is its newsprint,
billowing out like sail
or lyre, so thirled to his
sedentary form his head
is simply headlines, leader
articles, ads for the Arrow
shirts and collars we illustrate.
Illustrations, that's all we are,
and if there's 'lustre' or
'illustrious' embedded here,
there's also 'lust' and 'ill'.

Well, we're Big Sixes,
Joe College and Joe Yale,
cat's pyjamas, whiskers, meow,
the butterfly's boots
to the baby vamps
and bug-eyed Bettys
who write to us in thousands
every week. I mean we're
just sketches, Doll, all
dolled up in shantung silk,
sacque suits for summer,
choice bits of calico in our way.
You can have us in crash motor
coats, dust proof and durable.
Our bosoms pack these backless
waistcoats with a swell
that well sets off the Earl

and Wilson semi-stiff.
We never crease;
our bit of flannel's imperturbable.

None of my beeswax, but
do I know you? You stare and stare
and before you turn
away to go to bed, glance nervously
at the book face down
between my full-back hands.
Then you kiss our gloss.
We never seem to notice though;
Joe never makes
his point about the market.
But if you didn't go to bed
what then? Would it be
a fashionable tale or a tale
after our fashion? Would it
go like this: boy loses girl,
searches for her to the ends
of earth, turns round
at the last minute, loses
her again and here we are
in this upholstered limbo,
shades of our former selves?
Maybe? I almost believe
the story. Joe does, don't you
Joe? Though we can't quite
get it right; like it's in a language
we never fully understood and so
we turn from one translation
to another, like clothes
at a fashion shoot,
mugging up in case they
ever question us.

Once, we compared versions:
My lines go like this:
"And when suddenly
the god stopped her and, with anguish in his cry,
spoke the words: *He has turned round* –
she understood nothing and said softly: *Who?*
Never mind the god's identity.
I try, I am trying to remember
if that pause after the deft colon
was really there, and was it
her's or mine? Once Joe, you took
the book gently from me
and it came out a little differently:
"So that, when suddenly the God stopped short,
took both her hands in his and said
with pity in his voice: *He has looked back!*
she did not follow him, murmured: *Who?*"
In this one there are her hands,
his hands, pity, murmur, nothing
soft. Now there are just Joe's hands
and mine. Let's pull ourselves
together, eh Joe, my Joe, old Joe?
We're butch and beautiful.
Forget the girls?
They'll strip us limb from limb.

THE BACHELOR STRIPPED BARE BY HIS BRIDES, EVEN

after a portrait of Marcel Duchamp by Florine Stettheimer

If I place my eye to the peep-
hole in this rock, I can just
make out his head staring
back at me from the borders
of the morning. Light
suspends it, blinds me
as I again unpack the shadows.
Who would have gone with him?
In order to descend that never
ending staircase and pass
through the smallest crevice
he planed his limbs so they could be
closer to me at every moment.
He shed beauty like a snake,
skinned his retina so no pleasure
could take root. Infra-
thin rouge on lips was all
that told me he was there.
That and his suitcase...
an album with his latest
songs perhaps or space
for me...It was touching
if I could still be touched.
But I was an idea now
and when he turned to me,
wrapped in his coat,
it was just to share the thought
that two blue threads floating
from his sleeve could help
him measure chance.

What was he thinking?
I turned away, back
into the diagram of caverns.

Still, I see that head
in my mind's eye,
like a bicycle wheel
attached to a stool
spinning out the same
song, same thread,
same net. I raise
up my arms and slip
nothing on.

ORPHEUS. EURYDICE. HERMES.

after Rilke and a photograph by PaJaMa

That was a beach at Nantucket
– The Jetties, maybe, or Eel Point Rd –
I forget. In the haar, flatness has given
up and the boardwalk ends in steps
descending. He sits down in the middle
or near the bottom, not far
from the top in fact. You could feel
the sea welling up all around; it hung
above like a soft pumice stone
and if it falls he'll wash up
in its caverns and gouges, foamy
and silver tinted. Out of the photo
there's the hint of a watery sun.

There was a hill, going
down. And a bridge-like walk-
way and the sea, the sea hanging. Have I
mentioned this before?
And behind, the long trek
of white lattice over the unstable
sand. It was like…

They must have come down this path too.

In front, he looks skinny in his blue jacket –
he looks impatient; he looks straight ahead;
he looks hungry; he looks.
The Leica camera clutched in his hands
looks back. He senses it there now,
heavy, grafting away;

though he's in two minds:
one churns like an animal turning
in its litter, never finding
its point of rest; the other
rushes forward biddably to train
the camera and snap the shutter,
its click like a muffled yap,
a shuffle of falling screens
that close then open at the echo
of their plimsolls on the sand;
those two who will follow him home.

He took the picture…still…
he's in the frame.

*

No. Those sounds are just ghosts
of their shapes which jut
from the dunes behind them,
his collar snuffling the wind,
the wind dashing up to his back.
He says to himself, they are
there; says it aloud; she
has crouched down; he
stands a little way off.
If only he could turn round
just once or be this camera
seeing them all
(all would be exposed
so near the end)
then they would be real,
maybe all of them,
those two, behind him,
at least:

the woman, wrapped in a nurse's
house coat, her whole body attuned
as an aerial attached to the walkway;
an abandoned instrument, she points,
and there, hand brushing the struts
that bear their weight: him

a man, whose blintering eyes blanche
everything that spreads before him
and no sound rises, no note, no
cry, an emptiness deeper
than the horizonless beach.
The mist connects them
like a winding memory
in which the other man,
far out in front, is lost.

Together, they turned
and went back to the car park,
not daring to look at one another.
She, irritable, her white coat
trailing behind her; he,
wrapped up in himself,
gesturing now and again;
the first man ignoring them both.

Perhaps they tried to remember
each other's touch,
and sunlight, turning through
the fog, caught them
like motes of dust scattered
in the rush of light
streaming from a film.

Perhaps the shower stopped it,
loosening them all, letting them
home to their own selfish thoughts.
And when, suddenly,
the woman put out her hand towards him saying,
with sorrow in her voice: *Can't you
look back?*
he did not seem to understand, and softly answered
Who?

                    Anyway,
dark before the rain-spattered exit,
I or someone else stood. You could not make
me out. I stood and saw
how, on the single track over
the machair, with a sad look,
the woman turned to follow him
already walking back along the path
to the vast absent view, his footsteps
echoless, so gentle, so patient.

FELIX, JUNE 5TH, 1994

after a photograph by A.A. Bronson

You thread a sea with your eye;
each time the needle enters your flank
the pain composes you;

trees that hung your voice
among these patterns
wrap your quilt in foliage;

a dog barks through the branches;
a girl's arm passes like an oar
across the sunlit patches;

now your song kneels
at the river's edge
and will not flow;

your passport head is pinned in silk.

For one last time then, the images of Orpheus or Dustie-Fute
– as he was once called in these parts – coalesce. And some of
these images are appropriate to A.A. Bronson's 'memento mori'
for his late partner, the artist Feliz Partz: the dead man lies
wide-eyed, staring out at us, mouth open as if in astonishment;
but the quilts and rugs and pillows that surround and wrap him
vie equally for our attention. They remind the viewer of the
great AIDS quilt begun in 1985 which now comprises some
50,000 woven panels each one commemorating an individual
who has died. I say 'some of the images are appropriate' to
make clear that this poem is not new. It was first published in
1994, the very year Bronson made his photograph, and formed

one of the final pieces in a long sequence called 'Dustie-Fute'. This mixed original elegies with adaptations, fragments of newspaper reports that first documented the outbreak of a strange new disease, as well as snippets from a medieval herbal. The aim was to create a text that was as patchwork as the commemorative quilt and suggest also the complex network of conditions that combined fatally to suppress the immune system of those they attacked. The sequence is now almost twenty years old and the events it chronicles – the early years of the AIDS pandemic – nearly thirty. It is a time of anniversaries. In a moment I'll explain why I reprint it rather than try to write a new poem in response to Bronson's image. It is also a fact that I cannot get beyond this image in my overall response to the series of portraits I have been writing about. I was going to write: 'these personal issues', but there is a sense in which they are not 'personal' but 'general' and akin in this respect to Bronson's own form of art practice summed up by the name he gave to his collaborative work with Partz and Jorge Zontal, *General Idea*.

But first, 'Felix' himself commands more attention. The visual image itself is quite large and takes up a good part of the wall of any gallery where it is hung. I haven't made an exact calculation but it is probably about the same size as the individual patches that make up the AIDS quilt which are three by six feet, roughly the size of a human grave. To this extent, therefore, it is the most extreme interpretation of the quilt's function. Assuming Bronson made the image partly with the AIDS quilt in mind – and this is far from certain – I wonder whether his aim was not slightly satiric: while it can be overwhelming to experience the quilt in person its mission can strike the viewer as softly commemorative, particularly when panels are viewed in isolation. Pathos is the emotion most readily induced.

But Bronson's art here is more visceral. He does not deal in metaphor and symbol as the makers of the quilt inevitably do. He more or less gives us the body of the deceased itself, pinning it to the wall of the gallery. What's more, the 'itself' is still, uncannily, a 'himself'. This is because the image is not complete without the explanatory description, provided by Bronson himself, which accompanies the photograph. The whole work is a mixture of image and text. There we discover that the photograph was taken in the hours immediately after Partz's death, that in the final stages of his various illnesses Partz suffered from extreme wasting of flesh and muscle and that it was impossible to close his eyes after he had died.

In the years since then Bronson has given various interviews about his work and it has become clear that Partz was to some extent 'dressed' for this photograph and that it was a final act of collaborative art making by the two men. He has also spoken about Erwin Panofsky's work on tomb sculpture which he discovered after the photograph was taken and, although it could not have influenced the work itself, Bronson wishes to set it in the art historical context Panofsky evokes. In particular, Bronson mentions the late medieval phenomenon of the 'transi' or cadaver tombs in which an image of the deceased is presented as if in the process of decomposition.

Nevertheless, I believe that Panofsky's opening essay on Egyptian funerary art is at least as relevant and fits better with comments Bronson has made about the way Partz's life force seems to have drained off into the brilliantly coloured fabrics on the bed around him. Indeed, Felix becomes an Egyptian in this photo. As Panofsky points out, the ancient Egyptians did the exact opposite from what seems natural after someone's death. They opened the eyes and the mouth so that the dead might see, speak, enjoy whatever type of afterlife was available to them. And they tried to make the dead happy by providing the necessities of food, drink, locomotion, service, all placed within the shelter of tombs that were often constructed as if they were houses.

So, if you look closely at the photograph you will see that Felix lies just within reach of some of his favourite gadgets and personal items: his cigarettes, his tape-recorder, the remote control for the TV, all objects that will come in handy in the millennia ahead.

Bronson closes his explanatory description with the following invocation: *'Dear Felix, by the act of exhibiting this image I declare that we are no longer of one mind, one body. I return you to* General Idea*'s world of mass media, there to function without me.' General Idea* in this context perhaps bears some relation to Egyptian *Chū* or, as Panofsky expresses it, *general world-soul.* So Bronson's photo is not so much commemorative as what Panofsky calls 'prospective' or 'projective'. Like the ancient Egyptians, Bronson knows that Felix still has work to do in the afterlife.

Bronson and his partners were brave men, saddened but heroic in the way they made use of their bodies in their art right up to the last possible moment and beyond. They are defiant and upbeat, certain that their art is of central political importance to the age they are living and dying in. They live with the daily spectacle of death and don't accord it too much respect. When something is as commonplace as that, you don't. It becomes a kind of tool of the trade.

For those of us who survive to contemplate this image twenty years later, however, some of the immediate political impetus that the photo itself attempted to galvanize and which formed its conditions of reception, has dissolved. The return of Felix to the General Idea allows other associations to cluster around it, many of them existential. For this image remains a 'portrait' and in any portrait it is the eyes of the sitter that give life, that focus attention. Felix's eyes are dead *and* open; and it is in this conjunction that the uncanny force of this piece of visual art resides. Indeed there is something puppet-like about his general demeanour and it was to Hoffman's doll, Olympia, that Ernst Jentsch turned in his initial attempts to theorise the uncanny, that unsettling mixture of strange and familiar.

A little later, the French philosopher of excess, Georges Bataille, would remind his readers of Robert Louis Stevenson's 'exquisite' definition of the eye as 'a cannibal delicacy', 'the object of such anxiety that we will never bite into it'. Bataille goes on to evoke the final illustrations of J.J. Grandville made shortly before his death. These depict the figures of a nightmare in which a disembodied eye observes a criminal who strikes a tree in a dark wood believing it to be a human being and from which human blood certainly flows. Again perhaps, a vision of 'Felix' as a broken and dismembered Dustie-fute and a tortured echo of the Rilkean tree that 'surges' in the listener's ear floats to the surface.

Above all, though, it is the embodied nature of Bronson's 'Felix' that most disturbs, a body that is dead and yet in which the traces of life remain visible. It fascinates precisely because it presents us with a view of what we most dread and most desire to see: to describe this as 'an image of our own death' is not quite right. Nor is it an image of passage or transition despite Bronson's evocation of the 'transi'.

It is rather the way in which the photo makes death present to us as it can never be in life. Think of Dr Donne having himself painted in his shroud, although there Donne 'plays' at death while Felix multitasks in a much more profound manner. We touch here on the still controversial Freudian idea of the death drive that helps to explain the repetitive actions and dreams of the trauma victim. When we catch Felix's gaze in this photograph what we see, then, are the bars of a prison that has held humanity captive from the moment it understood that it was mortal and desired a literal view of that mortality.

However, this still does not account for the full power of this visual image. And it seems to me that we cannot fully appreciate it without placing it within a specific historical moment which is the earlier catastrophic phase of the auto-immune deficiency syndrome.

The uncanny nature of Felix's gaze stems also from our knowledge that his deathbed was also the bed of love. I realise that this kind of remark could take us into the morally threadbare and intellectually puerile world of sociological commentary in which obscene equations were once made – and in some countries of the world continue to be made – between plague and homosexuality. My purpose in saying this, however, is simply to suggest the way in which this photograph both feeds and feeds off a century of Freudian speculation about the connection between *eros* and *thanatos*. In this respect the photograph delivers a shock of recognition: our lives and our deaths are made simultaneously present to us and held out to us, offered by Felix's gaze.

Shock and an image of prison bars were also present in my mind and that of many of my contemporaries in the early 1980s as we read the first reports of what would become known as AIDS and gradually took stock of what this meant for our love-lives and for our lives.

At that time, I spent quite a few years living in Paris researching the life of an eighteenth century oddball called Joseph Joubert. My days were mostly spent in the old Bibliothèque nationale in the rue de Richelieu, occasionally noticing the bald pate of Michel Foucault who often sat in an area of the library called the 'hemicycle' which was reserved for the study of rare books.

I was a much more timid figure than Foucault and this timidity may have saved my life at the time. Gradually, I became more politicised and towards the end of the eighties left the shelter of my libraries to take part in activist protests. I won't ever forget the one organised by ACT-UP when a whole crowd of us sat down in neat rows, one behind the other, on the Boulevard de Sebastopol. We were carted off, surprisingly gently, by the CRS, the French riot police, and taken to the local nick where I was let go after a couple of hours. No-one spoke harshly or insulted us but I did notice that the police never took off their gloves.

Another image that remains from those days is a visit – several visits if truth be told – to a notorious bar just off the rue de Rivoli. I must have been all of nineteen at the time but the definite chronology of these years is blurred for me now. Downstairs, it was just a noisy, crowded bar. After I had managed to buy my 'demi' and been smiled at ironically by the handsome barman, I stood right at the back just watching what was going on.

Eventually I spotted what I hoped I would see: now and again men would nonchalantly stroll up some stairs at the back and disappear behind a curtain. More men went up than came down and it took me several visits to pluck up the courage to follow them.

I found myself in quite a large space divided up into different rooms by partitions and curtains. It was pretty dark though my eyes adjusted eventually to all but one of the rooms which was pitch black. I remember standing on the threshold of this room and trying to make out what was going on inside.

At first I thought it was empty but after a while I realised that something was breathing or sighing. I became aware of sound first of all and then, now and again, I made out the glimmer of an arm or a leg rising or falling. The room was filled to bursting with a mass of heaving, undulating human flesh.

Looking again at 'Felix' lying on his quilts, I can't help wondering if that glimmering darkroom could not be seen as a kind of reverse image of Bronson's photograph: moving limbs – this time – caught up in acts of ecstasy that morphed suddenly into immediate stillness. Again, I know that saying such things takes us into the forum where homosexual 'promiscuity' is 'punished' with death.

But such thoughts and statements belong to a different order of commentary. What we are dealing with here is not 'promiscuity' but an uncanny 'proximity' that characterizes ontology itself. In that room, as in this photograph, life and death commingle as intimately and as naturally as light and shadow.

But that decade of discovery was also a moment of imprisonment: the realisation that we would spend a lifetime – those of us who were lucky – of living at one remove (the remove of latex) from the most immediate and intimate expression of our love for other human beings. Unless, of course, we were willing to take continual, and for very many years, immeasurable risks. Not that I was as 'marked' as those contemporaries who did not survive of course. I have enjoyed a much longer lifetime than they.

But this is why I cannot honestly get far beyond the art of Wojnarowicz, of Mapplethorpe, of Haring or Bronson, cannot respond with poems to all those playful, postmodern, sometimes joyful sheddings of identity that characterize the final images of the exhibition, *Hide and Seek*.

I do not say any of this in a pessimistic frame of mind. My accent here is not intended to be calculatingly tragic. I am simply trying to understand and articulate the nature of an existential experience. The fact is that I was caught by that era; I would say 'branded' almost, in all senses of that word.

And there is a sense in which everything since the early 1980s has been a strange kind of 'afterlife'. Is it right or sensible to make so much of that basic, sexual act? From every rational perspective, from every emotional perspective – in terms of what we owe to our families, friends and existing partners – no. But to write a new poem based on Bronson's image would involve a form of repetition of something that cannot be repeated, cannot be copied because it always accompanies you at some level of your being and because that 'original' poem is always happening, always being said.

I was going to admit to a kind of artistic impotence here but I have come to believe that there are some essential experiences – among them this experience of the prison – that you carry with you, that you constantly although not always consciously inhabit and that rather than attempting to 'transcend' them and 'move on' – to use the threadbare vocabulary of the agony aunt – it is better simply to remember them and, if poetry is at issue, to recite them. Recitation is not the same as repetition.

Bronson's photograph shows us something very primitive. Felix's astonished face admits to both horror and joy. He is Egyptian and he is extinction. He is the prison gate, one side of which is opening, just as the other is closing.

Muhammed texts me on *Scruff* from Alexandria.
I mention Cavafy and he asks me when I'll visit.
I think of Egypt, Shakespeare. *Never,* I reply,
It's too far. Then I clock he means the one
in West Dunbartonshire and blush. *Cavafy
was Greek,* he says. *I'm Syrian and a refugee.*
Constantine Cavafy would have known just
what to say then from his careful room.
He dealt in exiles mainly, some refugees
and had a knack for letting the window veil
blow back at the turn of a line
so we can see young Antony
glint briefly from his high abandoned
tower block, sense his fate blow out
along the second-best streets
of a second-hand city. Muhammed
is waiting for me to reply as I write
this poem. It is nineteen and a quarter
miles from Glasgow to Alexandria.

SARAH

Angels are good for a laugh; they come up
and they say: 'God will give you a child.'
I laugh and I say: 'I'm ninety!'

They stand up indignant, unfold their wings.
'You can't laugh at God', one says.
I laugh and I say: 'I'm ninety!'

They leave in a flap and I have a wee boy
called Isaac whose name means 'he laughs'.
I laugh and I say: 'I'm ninety!

but his nappies need changed and he giggles a lot'.
Life's been a laugh despite all the travel.
Abraham gave me to Pharaoh, then Abimelech,

passing me off as his sister. Even at ninety
I'm pretty enough to tempt rulers to slit
my old husband's pendulous wattle.

At tea-time each night we laugh at our names:
'Mother and Father of multitudes'.
I'm ninety and he's ninety-nine.

THE LEVITE'S CONCUBINE

When they raped me, they said I was second best.
All along I knew it was him
they fancied, my young husband. Our host
wouldn't have it. They could take his virgin
daughter instead but not a man who'd shared his house.

My husband, my young husband, wouldn't hear
of that. He thrust me forward and slammed the door.
I am his second wife. Now he is preparing
to cut my used-up body into twelve equal parts
to send among the tribes of Israel.

They must pay him for his sacrifice. I recall
our wedding day: how his first wife gave me to him,
a far off look in her eyes, as if she saw
our husband moving further and further away,
a man, firmly out of reach, summoning his God.

MARY MAGDALENE

What I remember is a terrible dream
of something hanging nearby, above me,
just to the right and I couldn't look up.
There was blood. The whiteness was tremendous.

What I remember is that I was weeping,
and I turned to the gardener — who looked like
my husband — and I screamed, 'The body has gone!'
He told me to look inside. 'Look within.'

Two words. So I think he meant into myself.
I tried but found nothing. Their questions
never stop. I feel my bones going off
to preach on their own, each one with a slightly

different story. Some days I wear a red dress,
sit with my alabaster jar, to bring it back,
even the sins. They write it all down.
But what good will that do?

'Start again', was his favourite saying.
He didn't bleed.
The whiteness is tremendous.

Hebrew Women, apostles of Christ Jesus to Paul,
alleged saint, notorious scribbler: grace to you
and peace from God our Father. Now look here:

Adam could have said 'no thanks' or 'apples
disagree with me'. He didn't. He had a bite
as well. So he was deceived. Just like Eve.

We're equal and get used to it. We washed his feet,
made his tea, stood under the cross.
Where were you? On some road to Damascus.

Useless. Chapter 2: this new covenant is all very well
but we have a soft spot for the old one. That tabernacle
had our best candlesticks in it, a gold jar

with jam by Manna and a lot of tablet. We want
it back. You promise this and you promise that.
Be quiet. Let the hidden person of the heart speak out.

Chapter the last: every Tom, Dick and Harry's
given hospitality at yours in case they might be
angels. Fine. But haven't you noticed the spinning

saucers we've got above our heads?
Faith is a stubborn doubt before what you despair of
and the conviction of things you can see with your own two eyes.

WOOD

Heartwood in softwood thought of Adam
and the chair back it gave the young gardener.
Sapwood in softwood remembered the shadow
cast by the apple on bark. Springwood,
too young to recall much at all, imagined
the coming and going under the palm tree
at Timnah; and corewood still felt the essential
pain of being bush in a world thinking itself
divine. As latewood allowed a final
sparrow to take its last blood red berry,
they stiffened. Began to concentrate
on cell length, wall thickness, cellulose crystallinity.
Between them they wove their own myths
about moisture and fire. They never took earth for granted.

WELCOME, WANDERER

I know a bench that the sun strikes
at precisely 10am. At 10.02 I take my coffee
to the garden and sit for fifteen minutes.
These are my minutes. No-one else's.

A neighbour may come down, stand
gravely hanging washing and comment
from his distance, acknowledging
my freehold of this space and time.

But that is all that he can do. By
10.18 I am back inside and the garden
fills to the sounds of a little girl
chattering to her Dad. New neighbours.

They will reign there for much longer
but I will not grudge this; the young
are made for light. Next, we measure
flour for cakes and feed three spoons

of honey to granola. Later, I walk
the flowering terrace for forty minutes
and wish a beast of trig and math,
a hovering bird with violet eyes

more accurate than mine. It
drinks me from these sums.
Honeysuckle floods the air
with wings. Indoors again,

a bumblebee bumps up
against the pane and we go
straight to bed at 10
to get our eight hours straight.

We dream the same dreams
every night, dreams the same
as days like these, although
there are no numbers;

just the immeasurable space of avenues,
empty of cars and buses, people, hummingbirds.

SUGAR

These words should be unearthed.
They make do with all that oiling and caulking,
finicky odd jobs at last getting done
or the plonk plink from an open window
where time passes its life. They dream
of ambergris, castoreum, civet, musk,
— sweet, earthy, marine, animalic —
pomanders against the plague.

This aftermath is like 'la petite mort'.
But only 'like'. Words knock
on the bark of trees, barking
to be let back in. To the sugar,
the gravity, the heartwood.

CARVED WOMAN WITH STONE BIRD

The carved woman with stone bird at her breast
waits for the tube at Walthamstow.
She lost her first meanings a thousand years ago
and the commuters' projections bounce off her
with the rattle of the train or other stones
skiffed across water. Perhaps she has forgotten
how the man took the bird and it flew off
like glory; how he placed a child there instead.
Or how the bird came down again
and she was venerated once more.
Perhaps she has forgotten how the sea
once carved her and the bird to look like
a woman with a bird at her breast.
Perhaps she has forgotten how she lost
her colour or stepped from a frieze,
carved and cold and grey; how she almost
put childish things away, seduced
by our complicit smiles then drew
back into her real stone world
where a pebble is a mountain,
tree or person. She sits opposite us now.
The opposite of a sign. She is not a number
or a picture. She is not a story.
When she alights she is the pavement beneath our boots,
a stone in your shoe. She recognises
others as she leaves who have no roof
but the sky and how they too are stones
although made of flesh.

NATURAL

Good walls begin life quietly.
One stone at a time.
Protect us from creek maw,
its sudden yawn. My palm on our
wall's rough cheek, warm or wet,
it harbours us and the swallow nest,
small speckled eggs in crevices
behind the clinging grasses.

Each stone is a placed thought,
an angle of intent, of care,
worn and weathered thoughtfully.
No-one will insure it, slapped
by the sea which wears it
down daily, nightly. Our stubborn
house posts like a look-out,
a stone that looks out at the sea.

Our neighbour puts his feet up
on the breakwater and swears
at us: 'I know you, your kind.
It's not natural', he snaps,
swinging from his deck chair,
all poop and gob and bulwark.

He throws those stones at us.
In the sunlight. The wasps
at the Irn Bru can for stub-outs
in the window-box
are not disturbed.
And we split the stones,

make them fit for hearting holes
in this hard wall.

One day we saw the dolphins
leap over the breakfast table.
Often we cannot hear the slither
of green and silver creels
train their mesh upon the wash.
Once we saw St Adrian

kayaking his mortsafe
across the firth. Never,
the father of two who filled
his pockets with the millstones
of his mortgage. He walked
on stones right into the sea.

Wall pennywort, wall rue,
footings and fillings
and foundations
observe our living.
One man alone
could not lift the through
stones into the first
or second lift.
And now we heft
the lift above us,
coping stones,
standing in the blue.

THE MACHINE FOR MAKING EPIPHANIES

The machine for making epiphanies
is unsuspended
it hangs in space as Earth once did

before the second bang. Provenance
unknown, accession date obscure,
its 'isn't thereness' inflames

museum air; you move to kiss
it as a reliquary, your body
reflected in its silvery skeleton

but glimpse instead the straw
nest of a harvest mouse,
'micromys minutus',

leaves and stibble,
foggage green or ribbons
all stray and wisp about

the dark hole at its heart.

ITHACA

Once, the great statues lined the silk road.
Their names were 'goddess', 'lion', 'funerary
weeping girl', 'merchant with beard like an abacus'.
Pristine and worn from the wonderful journey
they spoke of their fine minds, the excitement
of time travel, without moving a single stone muscle.
They did not fear the bazaar of generations
which milled at their feet and glanced up
shiftily from age to age. Who could bear them?
Not us. Not any more. With their high
mindedness, their competence, their curled,
cropped hair. We cropped them. Down
they came, the many into the one into
the rubble, because at heart
they are stone.

SAVER

i.m. M.P.

Today my screen saver has changed its mind
and gives me reds, yellows: hills and a loch
with autumn swimming in it. Simple pleasure.

That strange painting you gave me —a square of pure colour
with the French words '*ocre jaune sur orange*'
picked out— before we parted.

And now —sixteen years later— I ask its meaning
for the first time. Does ochre plus yellow give
us orange? The first caves were full of ochre.

Prehistory painted with nothing else. In Wales
there is the 33,000 year old 'Red Lady of Paviland'
and egg yolks, canaries, corn and buttercups,

gold, humour, gentleness and cowardice
are yellow. The list seems endless. Ah,
here is 'yellow ochre' also, and we are back

again at Altamira with its lovely yellow
ochre horse. It carried us away from each
other; led me to this short poem for you,

too short, and so long after sixteen years,
and you to a sudden death by drowning.
Why ask its meaning? You shared

Earth's simple pigments with me.
We learn our meanings
from the words we have already used.

A DETAIL OF BIRDS

after The Journey of the Magi by Benozzo Gozzoli

We queue at the feet of angels.
Wait for the Magi to turn up.
Above, is their circuitous route
through the cypress-lit countryside.
The breeze, the snore of cherubim
napping on trees.

A menagerie of wings
flaps out the beats
of the song we are always
rehearsing. Halos
wilt in the heat.

These are well rehearsed gestures.
Painters and poets busy
about us for centuries.
At their best, our ornithological voices
have pierced human plumage
with cries that are almost like birds.

Now, the bones of the ark
shine through the shape
of the stable. The skeleton
of rain sheds its stipple
on treble and bass.

Mirrored in each jeweled
droplet, a miniature
angel ignores our departure.
We are queuing again.
Soon no-one will ever have heard or seen
a detail of birds.

HIEROGLYPH

Once, there was a bird that did not want to be a letter.
It threw shapes in trees, on walls,
chirruped of flight, sunlight beyond
the bestiary of any script.
A bird that did not change
its meaning when faced
with east or west — a bird, a disc,
a bird, a disc: the flowers of heaven, the stars —
refused to place
its head upon a human body
to become a god.
A bird that knew how pictures
shrink, tails or heads
which limb is chopped
until a simple feather
stands for truth.

MYSTIC NATIVITY

after Sandro Botticelli

If an angel...
If an angel stopped.

Stopped in the lane before our barn
or the turreted castle and turned

to embrace me — oh the hugs,
oh the stopping and stopping! —

I would brush aside wings
and shake his hand. I would

dance all the friendly angels
out of their domes, their stables.

Why even the seven small devils
clasp crestfallen hands

before heading to hell.
May I turn to you then,

— as the child
in the manger turns

from his swaddling shroud —
and unfold the wings of your palms

like a gamp. You remember the loosening rain?
The dull, earthly weather? How

we shared the braille of our lifelines,
those touching gifts?

Was this in our lifetime? Now,
loose the arm from the shoulder,

the right one, the left one, re-
member the hand, cross

the painting's meridian
just into the lane by the barn.

THE UNICORN RESTS IN A GARDEN

after the Unicorn Tapestries (1495-1505)

This morning I am packing a unicorn
into Iggleheim's crate. Its companion
died in a mythical time
before this confinement.
Now it journeys alone
fenced by high stakes.

Of course it is just a tapestry
woven from unicorn thread.
It folds like the best of us.
Then unfolds from the mind
like a poem. As I try to fathom
its impossible family, flotsam

from another world bobs up.
A friend sends pictures
from the desert of a bedouin:
a pack of gauloises, a tattered
rug, a threadbare mobile home.
His stare is the only journey

possible beyond township
and contested settlement.
Fit for a poem about unicorns
which folds away, its *millefleurs*
as sharp as skelfs.

THE TOWER OF BLUE HORSES

after Franz Marc

How do you make a tower of blue horses?
From a blue smudge in a coat in the corner of a field
one grey-blue winter evening, breath
smoke blue, hooves blue with sludge.
They stack up in your memory, all
the horses you have seen, not one
imagined. The three that spied us
trespassing from the blue horizon
of a hill and charged us so we had to leap
a fence, blue with fright and laughter.
The sad tourist donkeys of Valetta
plodding through jingle blues.
The gentle five-month old blue roan that carried me facing
backwards round the stable yard.

The people of the Tower of Babel had no use for horses.
Their words fell on red ears.
Franz Marc's *The Tower of Blue Horses*
was 'degenerate' to Nazis, and disappeared.

AUTOPSY

The animals stand around the body.
Two at the head, two at the feet.
Two on each side of the fecund ribs.
It is impossible to read their faces.
Mesentery and jejunum are divided.
The small bowel removed and read
for auspices. Now and again,
one looks over a shoulder
to the cave where their pictures were taken.
The fire in darkness. The shrouded light.
Shadows bigger than all of them agitating
on limestone walls, a sketch of deer
and blue-grey bison chiming
with the gift of morning. Now,
they turn to the heart
which must not be removed
and listen for drumming hooves
etched on ventricle walls.

TOBY

after Tobias and the Angel by Andrea del Verrocchio

I am a dog called Toby.
From a family that likes the letter 'T'.
Granda is Tobit —he's blind—
and my Da's his son Tobias
who strides beside the angel in this
very handsome painting by Verrocchio.
Though I myself, and that fish dangling
from Da's left hand, were sketched in by his pupil
Leonardo. They say he'll be a big fish some day
though he never finishes anything.
It seems I'm the only good dog
in the Bible though I don't recall
the names of any bad ones either.
I'm not going to speak about the angel,
Rafa. Big boots! He was
impossible. To keep up, I shook
a leg. You have to move it
twice as fast where angels tread.
It's clear. I'm sizing up the fish. In fact
I was trying to tell Tobias
and the angel about this man
I met, way back — when I was a trottery
little spirit— called Noah.
But it just comes out 'ark-ark,
ark-ark, ark-ark' and they close
their ears and eyes to me.
Indeed, I'm almost not there at all.
Thanks to Leonardo. Look! You can see
right through me to the grass,
the flowers! Ghost dog, my fur

sprouts like a fingerprint
on an access screen. Really,
my job is not to let my body
get in the way. A rather fishy tale.
Now, where have I heard that one before?

THE LIBRARY

The library fell. Couldn't it
stand forever, an open
book on the desk like a small
hawk absolutely still, balanced
on invisible thermals of thought.

Its excitement has torn
pages from itself; wing
by wing it grew in perfect complements,
author after author strung out
on its wiry, window-lit music.

The library has gone
indoors; to virtually
nothing; a match head
that won't ignite

a poem, the salt
of outside scratching
phosphoric words,
mouths hovering in air.

SAPPHO'S DADS

for Gerry McGrath

Ten different guys are named as Sappho's Dad.
It was 'Simon'. No, it was 'Eumenus.' 'Eerigius'?
'Ecrytus, then'? Not a promising start. Though
she was full of them. Until she saw Aphrodite
swim the whole length of the swimming pool,
and complete her callisthenics. Suddenly,
Sappho found the grace to confer an ode to her
— intact, entire — upon eternity.
Is this what Mark Rothko painted
in *Number 10*? The umber bloom a bathing
goddess stained all time with. Such buffed
spirituality. And in time it left her — Sappho —
sketchy, her lane in the abandoned
swimming pool scissored by the light.
Who looked out for her? Simon. Eumenus.
Eerigius. Ecrytus. Semus. Camon.
Etarchus. Scamandronymous. An odd
number. Scamandronymous? It had to be
him. Or her.

BALANCES

after a painting by James E.L. Dunbar

Apples speak to a tidy house my husband
often says; it's his officious way of talking
but then I wonder what their chat might be.
It can wait. All I wanted was to bake an apple
turnover. Two good cooking apples is all
you need for that but when the scales
didn't look as if they'd tip I added one
and then another. Life is best with balance
my husband often says but such uncanny
stillness was bizarre. I called in Weights
and Measures. They sent a lad
who fingered my late mother's
iron avoirdupois then licked his lips
and said the lever 'turned deliciously'.
I was struck by that. I walked right up
to the technology and placed another apple
on the pan. It didn't budge. I'd got this purse
of masses in my mother's will and swore by both.
I clinked the little nest down on the other pan.
I swiped them off. I clanged five ten decagrams
upon said pan but nothing moved.
The boy from Measures mumbled words
like 'torque' and 'beam'. I beamed at him
and sent him packing. My husband ambled
up and remarked it was a 'matter of perception'.
I told him what mattered was there'd be no
pudding for his dinner because his *belle-mère's*
masses had lost their weight. He eyed me gravely
returning to his chair. I was perturbed. Gravity
is not an apple's raison d'être. Fallen, plucked,

it cannot match the metal on the balance opposite.
It was at this point that I thought of God
and sat down straight away upon the kitchen bench.
I do not often think of God in kitchens.
I was vexed and put the mechanism
in the cupboard underneath the sink
fetching out meringues instead.
But I kept seeing apples accumulating
in the dark, an applequake on Mevrouw Ridlehoover
in the house below. My eyelids droop
beneath the weight of apples.
Then yesterday I hoisted the contraption
out and tried again: this time the pan sank
fast beneath the apples' weight but two
cast iron masses, then three then four
of fifty kilograms each could not recalibrate
the fulcrum to its balance; as if it sensed
the heft of Meneer van Leeuven's orchard
in my two sour granny smiths.
My husband laughed and said to aim
my iphone at it but I knew digital
would not do this justice. I thought
instead I'd get it painted. A hiatus
intervened while I interviewed
a whole guild of artists. All were non-plussed;
I did not want a still life or a hidden moral:
no baskets full of glistening asps to replace
the weights. Nor artful symbols to suggest
the painting's making or how apples
left too long touching one another
rot, like us. I wanted him
— and I insisted it must be a 'him' —
to tell my story and paint what I had seen
with these two eyes: a painted copy

of the result of all my heapings,
my shovellings of apple upon apple
my finger-staving lifting of hard
mass on mass to balance the stubborn
fruit in air and restore my equilibrium.
We placed the instrument of torture
on the kitchen table and I brought
an apron full of apples: I made
the painting for him and he started work.

VINCENTS

I arrived stillborn, bearing his name,
just one year before him.
Often, he visited my grave. In his mind.
I became the ghost that painted:
single chairs and single beds; the mixing
and the mixing to get that cypress
that went up like a tomb in flames.
It all came out in negative. Even
the evergreen yellow.
That touch of greengown.

When I paint, he said, *I forget my body.*

So at last we found each other
in the wheatfields' whiteout.

THE EXIT

after Holbein's 'The Ambassadors'

A 'decagon', 'a torquetum', 'an astrolabe';
article after article stuck in paint;
the nations stacking their negotiations
behind a curtain of green damask.

Can you exit all the talk, escape
the map, the measurements?
Here, at knee-height a terrestrial globe
shrinks England to the size of Eden.

Borders twist like snakes across the sphere.
E G B D F. The Ambassadors build
their emblem. For each good boy
deserves his fun, positions

all the shadows of their stuff at cross
purposes to an absent sun. Are
painted standing in their grave,
this cabinet of things.

The anamorphic skull confirms it.
Itself the shadow of a shadow,
it stains the fine mosaic floor
and stretches, conductor

to a new perspective. To see it
bloom, one ambassador must step
a little to the right, towards the secret
bishop of his soul, move

all his paint to stand beside his friend
in the strange country of this portrait,
risking death to do so. He saw
death rise up from the floor.

We know what grew. We ask:
what diminished?

A WINTER'S JOURNEY

1

Margaret is a Queen. Does not
recall of where or who or what
or why. She sits and sits

in Dunfermline toun,
done up in insect paste
of lac and kermes,

crimson lipped, crimson
faced, sipping from a cup
of votive tea. At the bottom

left, there is the nurse
— supplicant — her apron
in flower of woad,

her mouth an O of
salad words. A scroll
of knitting trails

drop-stitched epiphany
in silver banderolles
across the miniature.

*

Margaret is a Queen. And this
the Black Rood Gospel
dry as a bone from its soaking

in a stream. Clasped in her bony
hands, she presses it
to remember why she must

remember. 'Do this',
the words just out of reach.
She presses

and in a capital
divided into storeys
her book nods open...

                    *

Nods open on Margaret as Queen
even of this thumb Bible,
— miniature reflecting back to miniature —

a tiny world of busy dustie-futes
hawking badges of her shrine.
There is her face again

smudged by night-moth
dust: a souvenir that can't recall
itself, that blesses,

remembers no-one's sin.

                    *

Margaret is Queen of the hospitium's
pressed flowers. No sticky notes,
or colour codes. No necklace

of alarm. But ghosts of herbs
and plants that scent
her way through life.

Lint in the bell and blue-blauers
from her childhood. Dew-cup,
dent-dy-lion,

minuscule leaves
of history so distant
they barely make her story.

Margaret is a Queen in Dunfermline
toun. She knits, she weeps.
Dry-eyed, she presses flowers

between the quires of gospel
pages, a black snow of words.

2

Campanulaceae: of the bellflower family. *Heterocodon rariflorus*:
a British Columbian annual herb. According to my *Reader's
Digest*, he would have seen this on his journey from pahhandle
to alpine meadows. Inflorescence of lax, solitary flowers borne
opposite the leaflike bracts; calyx lobes veiny, egg-shaped;
corollas of upper flowers, tubular bell-shaped, blue. I could live
in just one of these words all day.

Thermal cracking and slumping, due to subversion of the
glacier by a melt stream, may be responsible for the splitting
of Kwädäy Dän Ts'Chíni's body into upper and lower pieces
and the ultimate orientation of these pieces. In Southern
Tutchone, the language of his descendants, his name means

'Long Ago Person Found'. I saw his five hundred year old hat first. Broad-brimmed. A pilgrim hat.

Columbia needlegrass; flowers: inflorescence a narrow panicle, 9-36 cm long, the branches straight, appressed to ascending, glumes 6-12.5 mm long, smooth. The hairs are 0.2-0.5 mm long, the tips minutely lobed, membranous. My eyes close among all the figures. A leaf falls. He would have stepped on this, his shoulder-length black hair swaying.

Charged by the elders, Kwädāy leaves the village at sunrise. He steps quickly over the felt-like nap that stabilizes silt. Then he scrapes moss with his knife and places it in his scrip. Next comes scouring rush and fireweed, dryas, alder, willows, then spruce, and hemlock forest. I think Caribou, moose, Dall's sheep, a mountain goat, numerous small waterfowl observe him pass by. Maybe wolverine. But I cannot see this creature. He is very fit and may travel thirty miles in a day. I cannot think what he is thinking. He is a young man quickly walking. Sometimes climbing.

The find area is halfway between the aboriginal settlements of Klukwan and Klukshu. The remains were found melting out of an aeolian feature that had barely moved in centuries. The harp-like patch of snow he fell on was clearly visible in aerial photography that day. He fell on the harp of snow. And the snow harp held him in its clasp.

Listen to this! Saltgrass Distichlis spp.
Sandwort Honckenya peploides
Sea lettuce Fucus spp.
Sea lovage Ligusticum Hultenii
Skunk cabbage Lysichiton americanum
Sloughgrass Beckmannia spp.
Snakeweed Polygonum spp.
Spike rush Eleocharis spp.
Sweetgale Myrica spp.

Spike rush! Sweetgate! These words carry me through my day. Tiny rafts in the stream of thoughts. I grip tight but sometimes they dissolve beneath me like snow. They were all part of his world. We have not established the names of these plants in his language. Microscopic examination of fish scales on his beaver skin cloak reveal that he had recently eaten salmon. No fewer than five types of salmon (sockeye, coho, chinook, chum and pink) are found in the Alsek/Tatshenshini system. I can still make phrases. Though most are of the *Digest*'s making. My eyes pronounce them silently.

The forest falls away, then the alpine meadows. A whole field of little coloured dots. The air has a tang to it. Pine needles. Resin. Like Calais Muir Woods near Dunfermline when I was a child and every passing tangle hid the treasure of my future. He wraps his beaver pelts around him. It is cold and he ascends into the pass between the glaciers. He stoops, cups meltwater in his palms, sups and then spits it out. The day rises above him like a splitting headache. The sun is very high and the blue air transcends through layers of thinness. To his left and right there are nunataks which the *Reader's Digest* describes in a footnote as 'isolated peaks of rock projecting above a surface of inland ice or snow.' He stops again and examines the ground. He is checking the snow. I relish his day. His travel. His being among the snow and the nunataks. This new word I have learned. Does it matter where he is going? Shrine? Errand? Love? How this landscape has been shaped to these possible ends?

Figure 3 shows the location of the human remains on the glacial ridge looking east. It is like a silvery miniature of the kind I am sometimes depicted in. The lower part is in the ice on the far side of the person kneeling on the left. The upper part is in the ice beneath the piled fur garments which can be seen as a stain on the crest of the ridge, and located exactly between the anthropologist and the glaciologist.

During recovery of the body, efforts were made to reduce possible contamination. We all wore sterile suits and rubber gloves. The remains were approached from the south and wrapped in two layers of hospital sheeting. We flew him to Whitehorse by helicopter and locked him in a freezer. A procedure for the respectful treatment of his body was established in dialogue with representatives of the first nation peoples, his descendants.

Here is a list of artifacts collected and their provenance in relation to the body: 1: Hand tool, possibly a knife and its sheath 2: Woven hat made of plant fibres. 3: Fur fragments, found on top of the body 4: A small bead. 5: A small pouch with hide strap. We assume this item is the man's personal pharmacy. We will not open it but I can see the plant seeds, the remains of herbs nestling close together in the darkness. Like a horde of private words we must not speak. It remains in the icy state in which it was recovered, and has been placed with the body. 6: a simple wooden dart. 7: a big wooden walking stick. A world of wood and ice.

He died amid the rock-and-rubble aftermath of a glacial romp. But he was a tree-smith too. He came from a place of alders and dryas. Sitka alder pin nitrogen in their root nodules and drop leaves that add it to the ground. This enables the spruce which eventually shades out the alder. A forest community begins. Leaf after leaf falls and turns to mulch.

Hi skeleton is immature and suggests this is a boy in his late teens to early twenties. A hand is entirely preserved and partially cupped. By the day of recovery the lower body had almost completely detached itself from the ice by thawing. The upper body was still deeply embedded in a vertical position in an ice crack; a headless man standing in ice.

His hair was long and black. The ice had pushed his staff so that it lay like a bow on the harp of snow. We never recovered his head. Here are some questions: how did he die? How old was he and what did he look like when he died? Was he healthy when he died? What had he eaten? Where had he travelled? I imagine…I have imagined…his scrip or pilgrim's bag contained remnants of moss and healing herbs. Were the herbs against headache? Against a cough? Against dimness of the eyes? If the eyes should water? As a salve? A salve for flying bane; for sudden eruption? They repeat the doctor's words to me day after day. This is the bravest eye-salve against eye-pain and against mist, against teary eyes: take feverfew's blooms, babie-pickle, bell of the brae; take lily and lovage; beat the herbs together and boil them in deer's marrow.

He is standing before me and looking from below his round pilgrim's hat straight into my eyes, creature to creature. I am sure I have met him before. Suddenly there is a 'whoomping' sound. Instinctively we crouch, look up towards the nunataks and beyond to the high walls of snow. Goose flesh pricks up on his skin. One part reflects substantial compression which has caused his ribs to bend. Both the head and right arm ended up above the chest. They would have melted out first. The limbs of this boy I once knew. Perhaps during one of the warm summers of our past.

He is standing before me on the ridge of snow. My Malcolm. Every sound here carries. A pressed flower falls from my book, its dry leaves fragment in the air and an avalanche of flakes envelop us. Which century are they speaking from? Is it me that declares we can hear noises, words, the sound of folk talking high in the upper atmosphere? Our courtiers chatter so. He takes off his hat and listens. We listen and we hear sounds like words falling, a fluttering like cards shuffling, and illuminations of snow detaching from the scrolls of sky.

His head seems to have moved down the slope, with the hair freezing into the ice. It may have been carried away in meltwater streams that run across the ice surface like rivulets through sand.

As the head moved did it sing: have mercy on me, help me, I ask, as I am clutched by danger as from a great sea, so that neither the mortality of this year nor the desolation of this world may take me with it. Shield the right metatarsals among the rocks along the edge of the slope. Be near me, uphold me, my treasure, my triumph. In my lying, in my standing, in my watching, in my sleeping. Release all my body's limbs sound, shielding each with an airy shield. Put thy salve to my sight, put thy balm to my wounds, put thy linen robe to my skin, my skull, my locks of hair which I, Margaret, of Dunfermline town, I Margaret name. My two gnarled hands, surely to my nape and shoulders be a charm of safety for my head. My head, brow and threefold brain; ear bone, lobe bone, neck bone, nose bone, lip above bone, face, all bone, temples, chin, eyebrows of bone, ears, pupils, irises; I name them, silently. All the names swim like salmon in my bony head.

The evidence suggests that the body ended up face downwards. He stretched out his right arm above his head as if he blessed the snow that took him, the forearm bunched so that his head rested on the wrist; how I sleep, like a stiff foetus; his left arm outstretched along his left side, the pain of even my thin arm resting on my abdomen. No place for it to lie. The positioning of the legs always needlessly crossed is consistent with this orientation, and shows that the person was lying slightly on his right side. Lightly I lie like this, waiting for sleep. I try to match the sounds and catch only half a word here, there. He falls, my Malcolm, with all the little words of snow he does not understand. 'Hin, hin, hin, toc, toc, toc, gog, magog!' He walks. He is. He falls. The snow covers us. The ice presses us tight. The words congeal. Our right arm, our left, our head…

3.

Long ago person, Margaret, lost
and found and lost again
in Dunfermline toun.

A little rhyme helps hold back
the ice   the storeyed letters float
free   meltwater bones

'air' and   'tree'
and   'snow' and 'body'
sole revelation

A procession winds
down the miniature's field of ice
arm shrine   head shrine

chasse for torso
fridge of stone
slate   dusted   clean

ACKNOWLEDGEMENTS

Thanks are due to editors of the following publications where some of the previously uncollected poems in this book appeared: *The Dark Horse, Painted, Spoken, PN Review, The Hunterian Poems* anthology, *Versopolis, Write Where We Are Now.* The poems in the *Iggleheim's Ark* sequence first appeared as a pamphlet from Stewed Rhubarb Press. The poem, 'A Winter's Journey' draws on a variety of sources including Beattie, Owen, et al. 'The Kwädāy Dän Ts'chíhi Discovery From a Glacier in British Columbia. *Canadian Journal of Archaeology* vol. 24, no. 1, Canadian Archaeological Association, 2000 and Alexander Carmichael's *Carmina Gadelica.* A special thanks to my friends in poetry for helping to make these better poems.